POETRY FOR THE ACTOR

a guide to deeper truth

To Matt and Kelly
with love.

POETRY FOR THE ACTOR

a guide to deeper truth

SELECTED AND WITH AN INTRODUCTION BY

DEBORAH HEDWALL

A Smith and Kraus Book
PO BOX 564, Hanover, NH 03755
Editorial 603.643.6431 To Order 1.877.668.8680
www.smithandkraus.com

Manufactured in the United States of America.

ISBN: 978-1-57525-949-9
Library of Congress Control Number: 2020933218
Typesetting and layout by Elizabeth E. Monteleone
Cover and cover photograph: Costa Boutsikaris
Glacier National Park, Rocky Mountains, Montana, USA. 2019

For information about custom editions, special sales, education and corporate purchases, please contact Smith and Kraus at 603.643.6431 or editor@smithandkraus.com

for

Betty Jo, Lee, and Sofia — unfinished poems

ACKNOWLEDGMENTS

It is with deep gratitude that I thank the following for their contribution in the making of this book; Nina Boutsikaris for her constant support, research and patience, Costa Boutsikaris for his vision and skill in imagining the book cover, Kumiko Konishi for her invaluable skills in organizing the poetry, to Susanna Styron for her friendship and support, to Marisa Smith for her clear advice as to how to pull it all together, to Pete Kraus for his aesthetic eye as we designed the book cover, to Jurgen Jones for his help in an early draft of the introduction, and to The Living Poets Society whose members have contributed to this collection, I thank you all.

A very special special thank you to all the actors who for over 40 years have offered up poetry at HB Studios, Ensemble Studio Theater Summer Retreats in Lexington, New York on the barn porch, all the actors in various conservatory programs in and around New York, the Olmaians Summer Acting Retreat in Tuscany, Italy and the constantly growing and amazing studio actors at dh&co in New York City. You are the wind in my sails. I will be forever grateful to Vicki Kennedy for her inspiration and to my high school drama teacher William Crossett who said to me, " You are an actor. Don't be afraid."

To my children Nina and Costa who from the moment you were born have been my daily poems. To my sisters Ramona and Kristin for your unconditional sisterhood.

And to Maria Gabriele Baker, who if not for you, this book would only be a few scribbled words, left to sit on the "maybe someday" pile. You have the patience of an oak tree. My gratitude is beyond language.

I also want to thank any one who reads this book, may you find comfort in the universal truth of poetry.

ACKNOWLEDGMENTS

CONTENTS

II LOVE

III FAMILY

IV WISDOM

VI OUTRAGE

VII LONGING

VIII DEATH

Poetry For The Actor

a guide to deeper truth

INTRODUCTION: I MADE THIS BOOK BECAUSE

I made this book because I believe that actors can benefit enormously by incorporating poetry into their personal lives and, by extension, into their creative practice and process.

I have been an actress and teacher of acting for 40 years and as long as I can recall I have been searching for guidance in an often confusing world. I look to the theater to be one of the last bastions of truth telling and that actors, the messengers of the human experience, must be held accountable to convey those deepest truths. They must be unafraid and curious about the emotional wilderness set before them, capable and fearless to breathe life into the exploration of human experience. By its very nature poetry encourages quiet contemplation, focus, and brave self-reflection, that expands the heart and mind to ignite greater awareness of the world. Poetry invites the actor to claim a place in the great history of the human endeavor that has forever struggled to make sense of love, death, morality, existence and the unknowable. The commitment to deep exploration of these themes forms the very foundation of the actor's work. Towards this end, befriending poetry can bring rich insight and emotional intelligence to the actor's craft. Most importantly, poetry can awaken an actor out of the doldrums of what is often a merely comfortable and literal version of life and bring forth a profound confidence in offering a more complicated, vulnerable and multidimensional performance.

I don't imagine myself to be a scholar on any subject. It's not my intention to determine what is good or bad poetry. This book is simply driven by my experience with poetry as richly informing the actor's creative process and emotional relationship to life itself.

As my work matured in both respects, acting and teaching, I came to understand that all creativity is driven by curiosity. An actor's ultimate responsibility is to connect with and embrace the vast landscape of human experience so they can live truthfully in any and all circumstances. That is the actor's job. A teacher's job is to help guide the creative artist to that abundance of potential. Poetry is the great voice of curiosity and contemplation that can serve as an invaluable tool to awaken one's heart and mind to endless possibility.

I began consciously weaving poetry into my life many years ago on a summer night when a friend and I were sitting in the sand in Cannon Beach, Oregon watching the crimson sun sink slowly into the Pacific Ocean. We were drinking whiskey. He was finding his way through a painful breakup and I was falling in love, madly and passionately, with an older guy who rode a motorcycle, had a gold ring in his left ear and wore his dark thick hair in a ponytail. Holy hell. My friend and I were both on the edge of ecstasy and/or disaster.

He read to me from the "First Elegy" of Rainer Maria Rilke's *Duino Elegies* and my heart broke open into weeping. My trepidation and fear of "falling in love again" fell away and comfort rushed in. From that point on I became curious about the resonating effects of poetry, both healing, disturbing and enlightening.

It would be in that late sunset light, listening to Rilke:

> Who, if I cried out to the order of our angels,
> would even hear me? And supposing one of them took
> me to heart: I would perish before their

> stronger presence. Because the beautiful is nothing
> but the beginning of the awful, which we barely endure
> and we admire it so, because it calmly disdains
> to destroy us. Every angel is terrible.

that I realized my appreciation for poetry had in fact been planted much earlier, and was waiting to be an active and conscious part of my creative life.

I was raised in the north end of Seattle, Washington in a small brick and cedar house my parents bought on the GI Bill in 1955. It was on a quiet unpaved road surrounded by a few similar houses and a dead end that opened up into acres of glorious woods where my sister and neighborhood pals had all sorts of camps, tree houses and even a dusty old abandoned chicken coop hidden deeply in a stand of massive cedar trees. I would often go to the coop alone with a volume or two of *Childcraft* poetry books. I was in love with the weight, the smell, font, the feel of the paper and the gorgeous watercolor illustrations in those big red books circa 1950.

Climbing up the rickety ladder of the coop I would curl up amidst old feathers left buried in the stinky straw and read out loud the poems about fairies, elves, magical dragons, the woman who lived in a shoe, the owl and the pussy cat who went to sea in a beautiful pea green boat, the elephant who tried to use the telephant—No! No! I mean an elephone who tried to use the telephone.

And then there was "star light, star bright, first star I see tonight." These poems transported me from the chicken coop in the woods of that dead end street to islands, ships, castles, jungles and oceans. Poetry awakened my imagination to the vast possibilities of adventure and experience.

At twelve years old the tsunami of puberty overwhelmed my life. Girls, boys, sex, sex and the myriad of distractions embedded in my hormonal storm left poetry high and dry on a dusty shelf. It was my junior year in high school, having satisfied a sufficient amount of sexual curiosity that I was able to return to my studies with any real focus and commitment. It was also then that I became acutely aware of the looming non-negotiable college plan set forth by my mother. All I wanted was to go to New York and become an actress but my mother had other *sensible* plans and convinced me that while I was in college preparing for a real job, in the real world I could certainly take "acting lessons." I did some research and discovered that the University of Washington indeed had a Drama Department that offered acting classes. That made things a little more interesting so I decided it would be useful to be as prepared as possible for the college entrance exams so I enthusiastically signed up for all the advanced courses I could manage.

It was Vicky Kennedy who first significantly changed my life. She was the high school teacher for College Preparation English with a concentration on poetry. My first class with her was September of 1969 and she had just returned from Woodstock, *thee* Woodstock, August 15-18. She mesmerized us all with her stories of three days and nights of rain, sun, mud, swimming "freely" in the river, music, music, music and I suspect a fair amount of mind altering persuasions. She told us about seeing everyone from Janice Joplin, Richie Havens, Crosby, Stills, Nash and Young, and Sly Stone to the final two hour set by Jimi Hendrix/Gypsy Sun and the Rainbows. I asked her how she got to Yasgurs Farm in upstate New York from Seattle Washington and she replied, " I had to go. And I found a way." I had never met anyone like this woman. She was wickedly smart, funny, beautiful, elegant, wild and utterly curious about life. We would spend the classes reading poetry out loud to each other and then we would discuss the likes of *The Love Song of J. Alfred Prufrock* by T S Eliot, *The Red Wheelbarrow,* by William Carlos Williams, *The Negro Sings of Rivers*, by Langston Hughes, as well as some of the beat poets, Allen Ginsberg's *America, Howl* and Diane Di Prima's *City Lights 1961.*

Ms. Kennedy would lead us with questions, encouraging us to share responses to what we had just read/heard. Her wise guidance would inspire and hold the attention of an entire room of teenagers, inviting even the toughest of boys and the quietest of girls to offer up their feelings and reflections. Most extraordinary was when she would bring our class to utter stillness, close her eyes and recite a favorite poem. To this day I remember her calm and melodic rendition of *The Lake Isle of Innisfree* by William Butler Yeats. She would end each class encouraging us all to write poetry, to express our deepest feelings and contemplations through written words. She would tell us, " You are all poets. Write."

Vicky Kennedy ignited my heart and mind, I was consciously falling in love with poetry. Still, I had no idea at that time how central poetry would be in my journey as an actress, a teacher, and a woman.

While I attended the University of Washington's undergraduate drama program, I was cast in a production of *Moon Children* by Michael Weller at A Contemporary Theater, (ACT) one of the few professional theaters in Seattle at that time and under the direction of Gregory Falls. As it turned out, I was in way over my head, and when the play ended its run Mr. Falls took me aside.

"You have talent," he said, "but you have no idea what to do with it. If you want to become a true actress, you need to get serious and study."

I left college in 1972 and moved to New York City, taking with me my savings of five hundred dollars and a handed down suitcase secured with an old belt and strapping tape. I was determined to find a teacher and begin my journey as a serious actress. Not having a clue how or where to live in New York I checked into The Barbizon Hotel for Women on Manhattan's Upper East Side. No men were allowed past the lobby, cigarettes and alcohol were strictly forbidden. I was busted after two weeks when Estelle the cleaning woman found a decent-sized roach in the ashtray and the two cans of beer I had stashed on the outer ledge of the window which served as a refrigerator. Magically the roach disappeared, (I have wondered to this day if she smoked it, tossed it or sold it.) but she confiscated the beer for cold hard evidence. Mercifully, the management simply made me agree to no more alcohol and I was given a week to find somewhere else to live. Through *The Village Voice* I found a small railroad flat, 417 East 60th Street, 5th floor walk-up, toilet down the hall with a pull chain, and bathtub in the kitchen—for $175. I wasn't sure how I would pay for it but I took a chance and signed a year lease. I scored a job in the budget sportswear section of Alexander's Department Store, which was just a few blocks walking distance from my apartment. I had never worked in retail and it must have been obvious to the management that I had no idea what to do or how to "sell" and so I was required to go to a three day training course to learn how to smile and appear interested in the customers. It was very challenging. The sales job at Alexander's was so tedious and mind-numbingly boring that I would spend most of my time figuring out how to steal stuff. Always prepared by wearing a loose corduroy jacket, I would select a few items, walk casually into a dressing room and layer the contraband within the jacket. I loved the risk involved, I was obsessed with taking as many items as I could. I also knew I *had* to get out of there before I got busted so I spent long hours after work walking the neighborhood looking for other possibilities. I also knew where the crowded bars were that offered "Happy Hour with Free Bar Food," so I would often duck in and pretend I was waiting for someone while I ate as much bar food as I could without drawing any attention to my hunger.

One early cold rainy afternoon in early January 1973, I found myself on East 54th Street in front of The Neighborhood Playhouse School of the Theatre, which was under the direction of Sanford Meisner. Without thinking twice I walked in and requested an appointment. The following week I sat waiting for my interview in Mr. Meisner's office. It was a dark room lit only by a few floor lamps and an old banker's desk light; the walls were covered in framed Playbills and photographs of Meisner with actors, writers and directors from The Group Theatre of which he was a founding member. I was enchanted by a beautifully framed portrait of the legendary actress Eleonora Duse and I will never forget how I flushed when my eyes landed on a quote, perfectly placed above the great master's desk:

"I wish the stage were as narrow as a delicate tightrope, so that no incompetent would dare step foot upon it." Johann Wolfgang von Goethe.

This was the coolest place I had ever been.

Mr. Meisner came into the room smoking a cigarette; he sat down and stared at me through his thick glasses for what seemed an eternity. He broke the silence by asking me why I wanted to study acting.

"I have talent," I said, reciting Mr. Falls' words to me, "I don't know what to do with it. I need a teacher. I need to get serious and study."

Little did I know my life was about to change forever.

My first-year teacher at The Neighborhood Playhouse was the extraordinary Fred Kareman. His guidance was simply the most exciting thing I had ever experienced thus far in my little life. He taught us the exercise work that had been developed by Meisner designed to break down the defenses that cause superficial behavior. I watched wide-eyed as my classmates and I began to let go of the armor and layers of protection that we had *all* unconsciously developed over years of socialization and trying to please—please our families, teachers, preachers and the endless line of peers we'd hoped would take a liking to us, choose us for Red Rover, invite us to the Birthday Party or offer up a special valentine. Kareman led us gently but firmly toward spontaneous emotional and physical freedom. Most exciting was the building of a solid foundation of moment-to-moment truth—practiced by doing the famous "Repetition Exercise" five days a week, three hours a day (we were also expected to practice the exercise after school for an hour every day) —that served as the basic principle of acting and from which I have developed my acting and teaching skills. Meisner's technique demanded that the actor listen, breathe, concentrate on their partner's behavior and respond freely, one moment at a time. Fully committed to the discipline, I began to trust my impulses. My authentic spontaneous truth was *slowly* surfacing unencumbered by superficial protection. I was beginning to experience the kind of freedom I so longed for and admired in great actors. And it was thrilling. Twice a week Meisner would visit our exercise class to see how we were all progressing. He would observe our work and often would throw his arms up in the air, knock over a chair, toss his ashtray across the room and exclaim:

"You are making this about YOU!!!! Acting is NOT about YOU, it is about what the OTHER guy MAKES you do. You are only a CORK in the other guy's ocean, just a cork in that beautiful energy ... THAT IS VULNERABILITY. The depth of your vulnerability will determine your aliveness and the kind of actor you are." After a tirade he would become quite still. I will never forget when he once looked directly at me and asked;

"What kind of actor do you want to be?"

By learning how to listen, to breathe, to receive, to feel and react without fear, guilt, shame or apology, we young actors began to trust—to the degree a 20-year-old is able to—our true impulses.

Most of all, Meisner constantly reminded us to expand our hearts, imaginations and creative thinking by encouraging us to find in ourselves those things human and universal. This instruction led to a series of exercises called Emotional Preparation: We were to leave the room, take several minutes (often agonizing) to connect with something specific and richly meaningful, enter the room emotionally full and begin the exercise or scene work. I wanted to be really good at this "emotionally full exercise" and the harder I tried the more locked up I became. One day Meisner barked at me: "Stop performing goddamn it!!!!.... Dare yourself to honestly live what is in your heart or find something else to do with your life, maybe being an being an accountant would suit you. As long as you *control* your true feelings you will be a fake, a mere indicator."

"Ok," I hit back, "but in my life I don't think I am a controlling—" He cut me off like a bolt of lightening.

"You leave your slimy little life out of this pure art." He ended with a flourish, "I don't give a damn how intelligent you think you are. I don't give a damn if you are head smart and can analyze yourself. It will never make you an actor.....to be an actor you must be *emotionally* brilliant."

And he left the studio.

I was utterly mortified and in an attempt to hide my shame, I skipped the group lunch and went up to the tiny school library. It was a wonderful musty old room, with overstuffed chairs and a few ancient floor lamps that cast a quiet light across its small but interesting collection of plays, biographies, essays, play bills and journals.

And on that dreary day, much to my surprise, I discovered a beautiful collection of Rainer Maria Rilke's poetry and had only to open *The Duino Elegies*…

> What remains for us, perhaps,
> is some tree on a hillside, so that we can see it
> every day; what remains is a road traveled yesterday
> and the stubborn faith of a long-time habit
> that liked being with us, and so remained and did not leave.

…and the tears flowed. I indeed had many unconscious comfortable old habits that kept me safe.

I was not afraid but grateful for this painful new awareness, coldly served up by Meisner.

Although Meisner's hard truth helped me begin to let go of another layer of protection, it was Rilke's compassion and understanding of humanness that helped me be gentle with myself as I sought to do so—and which made clear the path I needed to follow to become the actress and woman I hoped to be.

From that rainy afternoon on I read poetry every day. I carried volumes around in my school bag, stuffed in a pocket or tucked into my belt. I found used book stores in the East Village and discovered The Strand at Union Square. I collected books that I have to this day: *Selected Poems of Delmore Schwartz,* Sylvia Plath's *Ariel*, W.S. Merwin's *The Carrier of Ladders* (the front two blank pages of which I used to make a sign for NYC when I hitchhiked back from Boston in 1975), Emily Dickinson's *Collected Poems*, collections of Gwendolyn Brooks, May Sarton, Stanley Kunitz,

Langston Hughes, T.S. Eliot's *The Four Quartets* and Walt Whitman's essential *Leaves of Grass*. I memorized pieces from his epic poem "Song To Myself" so that the words would live in me always:

> I will go to the bank by the wood and become,
> undisguised and naked,
> I am mad for it to be in contact with me.

By weaving poetry into our daily lives we naturally connect to a greater universal truth. When we fall in love, fall out of love, lose a loved one, care about our holy planet and animals, are concerned about the well-being and safety of our children, dignity for *all* the people, recognize the horror and cruelty of war, the pain of inequality, injustice, racial and gender persecution, the suffering of poverty and hunger, we collectively experience the inevitable human journey. And poetry can help us embrace this full spectrum of emotions—from exquisite ecstasy to brutal despair.

At the end of our first year Meisner came to watch our final scenes. When we had finished we sat anxiously waiting for his response. He got up out of his chair, silently crossed the studio, cigarette dangling from his fingers, turned to us and growled, "You all need to have one devastating love affair before I ever see you again."

Perfect timing. I happened to be falling for a guy who gave me a book of essays and I stumbled upon the wisdom of Aeschylus, Greek dramatist of the 5th Century BCE:

"The truth has to be melted out of our stubborn lives by suffering. Nothing speaks the truth, nothing tells us how things really are, nothing forces us to know what we do not want to know except pain. And this is how the gods declare their love."

I was beginning to see that it is largely through adversity, heartbreak and struggle that we are able to become emotionally wiser, vulnerable, compassionate and more interesting human beings/actors.

That is what Meisner meant. Go get your heart broken a few times so you have some weight and depth to your work. Go get your heart broken a few times so you know what it is to fall to your knees in joy, sorrow, despair and humility. Go get your heart broken a few times so you can understand and embrace your humanity and extend empathy for others.

I proceeded to get my heart not just broken but shredded, more than a few times.

When I graduated from the two-year conservatory program in 1975, Meisner's last words to me were, "You're good kid—in twenty years you might be great. Remember it doesn't matter what you're *feeling,* it is ESSENTIAL that it is clear what you are *doing*. Fix your S and Good Luck."

I was a hurricane of feelings, Fred Kareman and Sanford Meisner had opened me up and taught me how to ignite myself into full rich emotional life. They taught me how to let my heart guide me and to trust spontaneous impulse and aliveness. They taught me not to fear or be ashamed of true feelings. I graduated thinking I was quite the actress. I had only to land a job and to fix my "S" and I'd be on my way.

Once out in the world, running around to auditions found in *Backstage*, it became more and more clear that I needed a teacher to help me *shape* all the emotional life that I had worked so hard to set free. I needed someone who could teach me how to create character, how to identify and make specific the circumstance, how to craft relationships, how to mine a text for clues, and how to use those clues to blend physical and emotional life into intention and action. I doubt I was actually conscious of *all* of that at the time, but I knew I needed some very wise guidance.

My search for that guide ended in 1976 when I found

Uta Hagen. Two weeks into her class I bombed in a scene from *Adventures in the Skin Trade*, based on a short story by J.D. Salinger. When the scene ended she stared at me for a long time and lit a cigarette. When she did speak it was to tell me I had no idea what I was doing, that my work was general and purely emotional. She gave me a few notes, but I had no skills or language to translate her critique so I remained quiet, nodding away. I left class quite shaken. Nonetheless, the following week I brought the scene back hoping it was improved—only to fail again.

Ms. Hagen grew frustrated with me and declared that I did not know how to work, that I was not ready for her class and "to please leave, now." I gathered my things in front of the entire class, crawled out to the waiting room and sobbed. Remembering I had a copy of Allen Ginsberg's *Sunflower Sutra* in my bag, I pulled it out and read its reassuring words:

> A perfect beauty of a sunflower! a perfect excellent
> lovely sunflower existence! a sweet natural eye
> to the new hip moon, woke up alive and excited...

I got brave. As the students filed out that afternoon I gathered up every ounce of courage I could find and went back into the room. As Ms. Hagen was collecting her things to leave I approached her bowed down and quietly asked her for a second chance.

Reluctantly she said, " You are not curious. True curiosity about every aspect of the relationship, circumstance and character is what brings an actor alive and leads to action. Period. Until you understand this you will never be an artist. Now get up. I will see you next week."

I studied with Ms. Hagen for the next five years; the last four of those years I was on full scholarship. I eventually got it. Curiosity IS the engine that drives the actor to understand truthful intention, action and connection to the other guy. She simply would not tolerate generality or the reliance on charm to masquerade as truth. She would constantly remind us of the brilliant words of Constantin Stanislavsky: "Acting is the reality of DOING ."

She would follow the quote by saying, "Nowhere does Stanislavsky or ANYBODY say 'Acting is the reality of FEELING.' Emotional life is revealed *through action.* That is it. Period."

Constantly, she inspired me to turn towards this excerpt from Rainer Maria Rilke in his *Letters to A Young Poet*:

> Be patient toward all that is unsolved in your heart and try to love the questions themselves, ...Do not seek the answers which cannot be given to you because you would not be able to live them. And the point is to live everything. Live the questions now.

Ms. Hagen instilled in me that curiosity is the only way to explore the energetic, emotional connection of the characters to the circumstance of the play. If you were not energetically engaged and in complete adjustment to the truth of the moment in your scene she would explode: "You have no true connection to your partner, you have no true connection to your heart, you have no need or intention, you have no history, because most sadly YOU HAVE NO CURIOSITY." Often she would end her passionate tirade with, "It is clear you have asked no questions. When you ask no questions it means you are quite satisfied and certain about your performance, and certainty is the death of art."

I had read and reread Ms. Hagen's book *Respect for Acting* and the second edition, *A Challenge for the Actor*—in my opinion, simply the finest, most clear instruction book on the craft of acting existent anywhere—and I was beginning to comprehend her definition of the serious actor: " He will learn to face himself, to hide nothing from himself, and to do so takes an insatiable curiosity about the human condition."

Well, there it is. Questions, questions and more questions lead an actor to clear action.

Over the course of five years Uta Hagen taught me the skills I needed to create and shape a performance. She would say, "A scene, a play, a canvas, a bare stage, a flute, a piano is just a lump of soft clay. The degree of one's curiosity about what to *make* of the lump of clay, is what determines who you are as an actor." She also never hesitated to add, "By the way, what you do with the lump of clay that is your life also reveals who you are as a human being."

In 1978 I was devastated by my young mother's untimely death. She was 51 years old, and though she had been arm wrestling with cancer for three years, she was living a vital and active life. I was fortunate to have been at home in Seattle with her and my sisters during her last months of days and nights. Six weeks after her death I returned to New York, but the loss of my mother and missing my sisters who were left in the aftermath was causing me tremendous anxiety and distraction in my classwork. The poor quality of my work was so obvious that Ms. Hagen was provoked to inquire, "What the hell is wrong?" I told her I was very sad. I missed my sisters. I missed the beauty of the Pacific Northwest. I was angry that my mother had died so young, leaving me and my sisters, including the youngest of us three, Kristin, who was a tender 12 year old with braces and pony tails, to go it alone. I was depressed that I was flat-out broke all the time. I told her all I wanted was to be on a soap opera—which apparently required very little talent—especially if a *certain* actress in class could land a part on one of these popular daytime shows.

"No you don't," she gently chided me. "A soap opera would kill you."

I started to cry. "I am 26 years old," I said, "I'm sick of working so damn hard just to *survive* in New York." I was unloading delivery trucks three nights a week for a rooftop greenhouse nursery on the Upper East Side until 2 a.m., I worked in a burger joint on weekends called Hole In the Wall, which was just exactly what you would imagine, where the most anyone would leave for a tip was one dollar...no matter what they had ordered; then there was the Christmas card factory on a West Side Pier at 28th street, off 12th Avenue, where I stood at a conveyor belt for 6 hours with three 15-minute breaks and a 30-minute lunch break. I had long hair, and was required to wear a hairnet that was more like a plastic shower cap, to ensure my braids would not get caught in the machinery. It was also mandatory that we wear a gas-mask type thing covering our faces because of the toxic nature of the glitter; so with a strange gun-like apparatus I applied the sparkly poison to the various snowmen, churches, Rudolfs, elves, Marys, babes in swaddling clothes, mangers, donkeys, twinkling stars, small churches in snowy pine tree forests, drummer boys, The Wise Men and endless varieties of Santa.

Sometimes I cleaned hotel rooms and stole change found on the nightstands so I could eat more than a container of yogurt for dinner and still have money for cigarettes. I lied about having had experience and was hired at a fancy French restaurant on the Upper East Side. I thought, "This is great, I will make excellent tips and get a free meal." I knew nothing about serving rich people who ordered expensive wine, and my French was limited to a few directional inquiries from my JIFFY PHRASEBOOK. I was fired the first night. A customer had asked me what the stuffed snapper was stuffed with. Dutifully I hurried to the kitchen to inquire. The chef 's French accent was heavy but I was pretty sure I understood him to say "hamburger." I reported back to the customer, who was so confused by my reply he called for the manager. The manager, embarrassed and apologetic, took over the order and told me to wait in his office. Thirty minutes later he walked in, told me the stuffed snapper was stuffed with a crab and a delicate herb mixture, handed me a 20-dollar bill and said in *his* heavy French accent, "Zees is not goink to verk."

Utterly disgraced, I grabbed my coat and snuck out the back only to find it was pouring rain and that my bike had been stolen, its chain cut and left smirking up at me from the glistening sidewalk. It was 10 p.m. and refusing to spend my 20 bucks on a cab I walked the 52 blocks home. Penultimately there was Under the Stairs, a pub on the upper west side. Because I was the new gal I was sentenced to the 6 p.m. to 2 a.m. closing shift. It was awful. The only thing that held me there was a pack of hoods who took a liking to me, some kind of unspoken protective authority I guess. They would pull up in a big black car and walk in like royalty, rings and gold chains flashing. Jimmy D would ask me if I had a dollar bill and I would hand him one from my tip jar. In return he would hand me back a 5 dollar bill perfectly folded into an envelope containing cocaine. He wanted nothing from me, but would just say " Anybody fucks wit you, le' me know, don't trust nobody, and get home safe." I would sell the the stuff for extra cash.

The night I quit a group of very drunk fun seekers came into the bar around 1 a.m.. One guy in high heels and a pencil dress was so tanked he fell off his chair and his wig went flying across the room. When I told him I could not serve him he screamed, "Get me a slow Fin Giz NOW BITCH," his bald head slick with sweat, smeared blue shadowed eyes bulging. I calmly walked to the bar keep, turned in my apron, pen and order book, collected my tips and explained to him that I was done and left. Not even Jimmy D was worth returning to the place. Ever.

In an effort to restore my battered soul, I spent the better part of the next day in Riverside Park with a volume of Emily Dickinson.

> If I can stop one heart from breaking,
> I shall not live in vain;
> If I can ease one life the aching,
> Or cool one pain,
> Or help one fainting robin
> Unto his nest again,
> I shall not live in vain.

The last straw was a so-called modeling job I found in *The Village Voice*. When I showed up to the designated address, the "photographer" asked me to disrobe. The studio was a bit odd, with a multitude of cheesy pin-up type photos and paintings on the walls of busty women in scanty underwear, wearing big smiles and full red lips. But I thought, well this is cool, like modeling for an art class. He started to click away and then asked me to sit on a chair and throw one leg over the very high armrest. When I objected he told me I had no artistic spirit and to get dressed and leave. Shaken I pulled on my clothes and as I headed out the door I asked him for the promised 25 bucks that came with the gig. He replied, "You did not fulfill the job request." He pushed me out the door, handed me a subway token and said, "Here, now get out and don't come back."

I spent the night reading *HOWL* by Allen Ginsberg:

"I saw the best minds of my generation destroyed by madness, starving hysterical naked...angelheaded hipsters burning for the ancient heavenly connection to the starry dynamo in the machinery of night"

Things started to brighten a bit when I got a call from a guy I knew from college in Seattle. He was in New York and casting a children's theater show called RAZZLE DAZZLE and would I like to be in it? It rehearsed and toured elementary schools in Huntington, Long Island. The gig came with three months of work, $200 a week, transportation to and from Grand Central Station *and* included, and this was the BIG *and*...the opportunity to become a member of the great bastion of professional theater, Actors' Equity Association. Finally, I was in the club. Hallelujah!

I left Ms Hagen's class for awhile and joined the circus. We were each required to play some sort of instrument. I was on washboard, spoons and kazoo. Barefoot and decked out in overalls and tie-dyed T-shirts we sang and danced to original music written and composed by the guy on keyboard. And while the gig lacked the gravitas I worked so hard to find in my theatrical training, it didn't take long until I was intoxicated with the guy on keyboard. When we weren't "touring" he and I took long walks in the spring time Long Island woods and beaches, stayed up very late, built bonfires, smoked the best weed I had had since leaving Seattle and ate a decent amount of peyote.

When the job ended the guy on keyboard tenderly broke up with me. Being a gentleman, he dropped me off at the train headed back to New York and explained, " We will always love each other, and it is important that we are both free." As I struggled to agree and smile through tears he tucked a book of poetry between my hands. *Twenty Love Poems and A Song of Despair*. Thus began my long and unconditional love affair with the great Chilean poet, Pablo Neruda. He would never leave me.

I will bring you happy flowers from the mountains,
bluebells,
dark hazels and rustic baskets of kisses.
I want
to do with you what spring does with the cherry
trees.

My heart bruised, out of work and flat-out broke, I rejoined class.

I told Ms. Hagen I was tired. I was sad. I was desperate.

"Alright," she sighed, "Stop sniveling. I am going to give you something no one will ever take away from you. I will teach you to teach."

For the following eight months I spent most days sitting in on all her classes, watching her every move, writing down her comments to students, memorizing her language and reporting back to her my understanding of how to constructively critique and talk to actors about activating, deepening, exploring, questioning and clarifying their work. A year later she bestowed on me my first classes. I taught basic technique using *Respect for Acting* as my guide. I had begun my first solo teaching endeavor in New York City at HB Studio, 120 Bank Street, Greenwich Village, New York City. Endorsed by Uta Hagen. I was in heaven.

Once having proved myself to be a competent instructor of basic technique, she promoted me to teach scene study. Possessing only a small collection of my own material, I asked Ms. Hagen if I could use her scene book—a gorgeous, well-worn, leather-bound book full of hundreds of scene ideas for women and men. She graciously entrusted it to me for a weekend. As I was poring over it, I noticed a section labeled AUDITION NOTES. Of course, my curiosity sprang forth and I found the page with my name on it. It read: "*Debra Hedwell...Patsy's monologue from Little Mur-*

ders....a very dull actress. Take only if short on women."

Apparently the class was short on women. I remain grateful to whoever it was who got a gig and pulled out.

As a teacher I understood and taught Ms. Hagen's basic principles: that acting is motored by curiosity that leads to the asking of questions that then leads us to action. And it is the questions that take us to a deeper understanding of the multidimensional, complicated, core of our humanness. If a student shows signs of talent, this approach works well and these principles can easily be absorbed and practiced. However, one cannot teach talent, and I often with first level actors I found myself resorting to the technical aspects of acting—akin to teaching piano by rudimentary exercise—or painting by painting by numbers. Consequent to this approach, many students would reliably demonstrate only the most literal and obvious understanding of character and scene dynamic.

Although finding gold in a dry creek bed can be challenging, to this day I continue to encourage anyone—for whatever reason—to sign up for a beginning acting class: Too many people go through life emotionally and sensually deadened due to various methods of soul killing socialization practices. To feel *something*, sharp or tender, to be brave, to look someone in the eyes, to spontaneously laugh out loud, to own a point of view and to voice it, to experience fear, anger, joy, or at the very least to push through one's emotional deadness and allow for vulnerability and trust your heart to speak - that is invaluable. These marvelous experiences do not necessarily make an actor, but they will enrich the life of one who might otherwise have gone unawares of their capacity to feel a range of emotions.

There are all sorts of exercises designed to help actors get in touch with and reveal deep feelings. Every teacher has their own technique on how to lead an actor to a strong point of view, and how to help an actor express despair, joy, rage, sorrow, ecstasy and everything in between. In my opinion there exists no one technique, that can guarantee an actor's true emotional release.

Struggling to find a fresh way to help actors discover and trust their unique unguarded truth, I began to reflect on how poetry informed my life and creative practice, coming to realize just how profoundly entwined my study of poetry was with my study of acting: Poetry helped me to understand that people have been wrestling with the same deep questions and moral dilemmas since the first storytellers were scratching symbols on cave walls, carving figures in trees, creating totems, dancing around campfires, honoring deities in birds and bowing to animals, wind, sky, sun, stars, moons, mountains, and rivers for guidance; and how it is that these same basic human struggles connect us all throughout time.

Our first storytellers were concerned with the entire spectrum of existence and that is precisely the responsibility of the actor. Plays are the written exploration and the messengers of these fundamental searchings. Actors are the fire-keepers of the stories, the sustaining flame of the searchings. And poetry is the language that connects it all.

Looking over my notes on poetry, I found an article about Franz Kafka, wherein he is quoted as saying, " A book should serve as an axe to crack the frozen river of the soul." Well of course! A poem can do the same thing.

The wonderful poet Lucille Clifton said, " Poetry began when somebody walked off a savanna or out of a cave and looked up at the sky with wonder and said 'Ahhhh.' That was the first poem."

For years I have referred to *The Makers*, a piece by the

astonishing poet Howard Nemerov, to ignite wonder and curiosity in actors.

> Who can remember back to the first poets
> The greatest ones, greater even than Orpheus?.....
> They were the ones that in whatever tongue
> Worded the world, that were the first to say
> Star, water, stone, that said the visible
> And made it bring invisibles to view....
> They were the first great listeners, attuned
> To interval, relationship and scale
> The first to say above, beneath and beyond
> Conjurors with love, death, sleep, with bread and wine.

In *The Language of Life*, Bill Moyers writes, "Poetry is news of the mind, news of the heart...poetry reveals a particular life to be every life, my life, your life."

And Rainer Maria Rilke offers these stunning words: "Poetry is the natural prayer of the human soul...to sustain and extend our capacity for contemplation."

And so it was that at HB Studio that I began introducing poetry at the beginning of every class. And of course, I realized that the spirit of Vicky Kennedy was fully present and alive. Just as she had hoped to, my intention was that poetry would help awaken and massage the hearts of all students, no matter the degree of talent. I read poetry and I required students to bring in poetry. After a poem was read I would invite discussion by asking each person to share what the poem meant to them. *What do you think this poem about? What is resonating in you after hearing this poem? What feelings are stirring? Did you learn anything or think a new thought after hearing this poem?* When I asked the presenter why they had chosen a particular poem, the *why* revealed a great deal about the person's world view, secrets, fears, shame, longing and dreams. That was exciting. Thrilling, actually. To see a person begin to think, *to feel* and awaken to curiosity, wonder and become aware of universally shared life experiences, was the absolute gold of teaching beginning acting technique.

It did not matter if they went on and followed the path of a life in the theater, became a stripper, an accountant or a nurse—still absolute gold. By encouraging students to read, listen and contemplate, I knew poetry could open locked rooms of fear, and that deadened hearts could be resuscitated and restored to aliveness.

One day a young man who had been studying for about six months asked if he could read a poem—I was pleased because he had shown little interest in our opening ritual. He was very thin and shy with terribly bad skin and always sat in the back of the class alone.

After he read "The Road Less Traveled" by Robert Frost, the class was utterly silent. Another student finally broke the stillness, thanked him for reading the poem and inquired as to why he had chosen this particular poem.

"I asked my mother if she had a favorite poem and she recited it to me " the young man replied. "She cried as she shared it with me and I had never seen my mother cry before. I learned a lot about my mother because of the poem. My mother says poetry is everywhere, in everything, so I am looking for it."

Another time, a quiet, introverted young woman brought in a poem about a young child surviving an abusive father. She was robotic as she read it. When she finished she closed her eyes and said to the class, "Thank you for letting me read this, it helps. My friend wrote this poem and shared it with me, we had the same kind of fathers." Many heads bowed and sniffles could be heard.

To my knowledge neither of these students went on to

be actors, but I have no doubt that each will continue to benefit from poetry and its invitation to embrace their unprotected feelings without fear and shame.

Over the past four decades I have taught in many acting programs, including BFA, MFA and at several two-year acting conservatories, all while maintaining a private studio in New York City. No matter what level, advanced or beginners, I have included poetry as part of the creative practice. It is how we gather 'round the proverbial campfire and remind ourselves that we are all part of the human story. Poetry is a contemplation that inspires curiosity about the mundane as well as the mystery of the unknowable, and advances our connection from birth to death to everything that came before and everything that continues on into the mysterious hereafter.

While we know there has been suffering and pain since the beginning of time, we are currently faced with unprecedented instantaneous reporting on the condition of the world, the violence in our country, in our towns, neighborhoods and, tragically in our houses of worship, music festivals, theaters, malls, parks, parking lots and schoolrooms. This inundation can create quite a dilemma for the sensitive and compassionate artist. We are reminded many times a day of the horrifying and unspeakable hardships brought on by gun violence, poverty, overall inequality, political, religious and racial persecution, gender-based hate crimes, as well as the constant assault on our magnificent planet because of corporate greed, avarice, corruption, mindless consumption and waste, exacerbated by many politicians that turn a blind eye to the earth's destruction in order to advance their own personal financial interests and accumulation of blood soaked wealth. It is easy to feel overwhelmed, dispirited and discouraged. What is a sentient being to do?

I remember when a friend of mine had a string of sadness—the sudden loss of his beloved companion followed by the death of his dog Micky, his house being burgled while he was away for a night, and his book rejected by a three publishers. When I asked him how he was getting through this very difficult time, he smiled and quietly replied, "I am reading *Dante's Inferno*. Poetry is perspective. Perspective is a healer, a gift passed on to us by the great witnesses of humanity."

Poets take on the universe of words, shape them, turn them around and inside out, they unravel them, color them, deepen them, explode them, rediscover and invent them. Poets very often contemplate a specific question or observation leading the reader to a new thought, a new awareness of something either never considered or more often, taken for granted.

Over these many years I have been collecting poetry—published, unpublished, contemporary and ancient—that has been instrumental in the expanding of my own heart and mind, the hearts of my children Nina and Costa who were raised on poetry, and the hearts of so many of my friends and students who generously share poetry and its infinite power.

This little book cannot contain so massive a collection, but it is my hope that you will enjoy these selections and be inspired to seek out more poetry. May you invite poetry into your life, letting its provocations resonate and ignite new thought, renew curiosity and awaken you to the entire spectrum of human experience freely and without apology.

Poems are not solutions for actors, they are simply sparks of light in the darkness that will not be extinguished.

This book is meant to be a portable companion—that might easily slip into a coat pocket, back pocket, into a purse or a backpack, the glove compartment of your car, or be secured under your belt buckle—designed so that it can always be there for you, encouraging your heart to be brave and stay open when life has folded it closed.

Reach for it when you are tired of being angry, when you want to forgive and be free. Reach for it when you need courage to be outraged, full of fire and wrath, when you must rail at the gods.

Reach for it as you wait in the long line at the bank while already late for an appointment, at the Post Office, DMV, car pound, or while stuck in bumper-to-bumper traffic trying to get to the airport. Reach for it as you wander through urban parks and sit under a tree, climb into an ancient cave in a desert, as you follow an arrow of geese flying in the sky, watch a hawk circling high above, or a squirrel hunting for nuts.

Reach for it as you hike a mountain trail and find the sun setting, as you build a campfire and look up into the starry dome, watching for shooting stars. Reach for it when you are lucky enough to watch the sun rise. Reach for it when you sit in a cafe alone on a rainy afternoon in February, enjoying an espresso, a whiskey or a slice of rich warm cake.

Reach for it when you are lying on a cement floor for ten hours with a heart so splintered you are unable to reclaim yourself. Reach for it when you are in a waiting room anxious for an audition or anticipating a determining or dreaded phone call. Reach for it when you are rehearsing, needing a new perspective and some courage to swim farther out into deeper water. Reach for it when you want to give up because you didn't get the job you *knew* you would get, the job that would *change* your life. Reach for it when you are falling in love again and need courage to say YES and jump. Reach for it when you are weightless with joy. Reach for it when life is difficult and you need to be reminded that you are not alone, that you are part of the evolution that is forever ongoing and now, that you are beautiful, that you are loved, that you contradict yourself and that you contain multitudes.

I. UNIVERSAL CONNECTION:

One's partnership with the whole world, before, after and now.

> "You think your pain and your heartbreak are unprecedented in the history of the world, but then you read. It is books that taught me that the things that tormented me the most were the very things that connected me with all the people who were alive, who had ever been alive."
>
> —*James Baldwin*

STANLEY KUNITZ

The Layers

I have walked through many lives,
some of them my own,
and I am not who I was,
though some principle of being
abides, from which I struggle
not to stray.
When I look behind,
as I am compelled to look
before I can gather strength
to proceed on my journey,
I see the milestones dwindling
toward the horizon
and the slow fires trailing
from the abandoned camp-sites,
over which scavenger angels
wheel on heavy wings.
Oh, I have made myself a tribe
out of my true affections,
and my tribe scattered!
How shall the heart be reconciled
to its feast of losses?
In a rising wind
the manic dust of my friends,
those who fell along the way,
bitterly stings my face,
Yet I turn, I turn,
exulting somewhat,
with my will intact to go
wherever I need to go,
and every stone on the road
precious to me.
In my darkest night,
when the moon was covered

and I roamed through wreckage,
a nimbus-clouded voice
directed me:
"Live in the layers,
not on the litter."
though I lack the art
to decipher it,
no doubt the next chapter
in my book of transformations
is already written.
I am not done with my changes.

JACK GILBERT

Failing and Flying

Everyone forgets that Icarus also flew.
It's the same when love comes to an end,
or the marriage fails and people say
they knew it was a mistake, that everybody
said it would never work. That she was
old enough to know better. But anything
worth doing is worth doing badly.
Like being there by that summer ocean
on the other side of the island while
love was fading out of her, the stars
burning so extravagantly those nights that
anyone could tell you they would never last.
Every morning she was asleep in my bed
like a visitation, the gentleness in her
like antelope standing in the dawn mist.
Each afternoon I watched her coming back
through the hot stony field after swimming,
the sea light behind her and the huge sky
on the other side of that. Listened to her
while we ate lunch. How can they say
the marriage failed? Like the people who
came back from Provence (when it was Provence)
And said it was pretty but the food was greasy.
I believe Icarus was not failing as he fell,
but just coming to the end of his triumph.

The Guest House

This being human is a guest house.
Every morning a new arrival.

A joy, a depression, a meanness,
some momentary awareness comes
As an unexpected visitor.

Welcome and entertain them all!
Even if they're a crowd of sorrows,
who violently sweep your house
empty of its furniture,
still treat each guest honorably.
He may be clearing you out
for some new delight.

The dark thought, the shame, the malice,
meet them at the door laughing,
and invite them in.

Be grateful for whoever comes,
because each has been sent
as a guide from beyond.

Sweet Darkness

When your eyes are tired
The world is tired also.

When your vision has gone,
no part of the world can find you.

Time to go into the dark
where the night has eyes
to recognize its own.

There you can be sure
you are not beyond love.

The dark will be your home
tonight.

The night will give you a horizon
further than you can see.

You must learn one thing.
The world was made to be free in.

Give up all the other worlds
except the one to which you belong.

Sometimes it takes darkness and the sweet
confinement of your aloneness
to learn

anything or anyone
that does not bring you alive

is too small for you.

Sonnet LX

Like as the waves make towards the pebbled shore,
So do our minutes hasten to their end;
Each changing place with that which goes before,
In sequent toil all forwards do contend.
Nativity, once in the main of light,
Crawls to maturity, wherewith being crowned,
Crookèd eclipses 'gainst his glory fight,
And Time that gave doth now his gift confound.
Time doth transfix the flourish set on youth
And delves the parallels in beauty's brow,
Feeds on the rarities of nature's truth,
And nothing stands but for his scythe to mow:
  And yet to times in hope my verse shall stand,
  Praising thy worth, despite his cruel hand.

TRACY K. SMITH

Beatific

I watch him bob across the intersection,
Squat legs bowed in black sweatpants.

I watch him smile at nobody, at our traffic
Stopped to accommodate his slow going.

His arms churn the air. His comic jog
Carries him nowhere. But it is as if he hears

A voice in our idling engines, calling him
Lithe, Swift, Prince of Creation. Every least leaf

Shivers in the sun, while we sit, bothered,
Late, captive to this thing commanding

Wait for this man. Wait for him.

We Have Not Come To Take Prisoners

We have not come here to take prisoners,
But to surrender ever more deeply
To freedom and joy.

We have not come into this exquisite world
To hold ourselves hostage from love.

Run my dear,
From anything
That may not strengthen
Your precious budding wings.

Run like hell my dear,
From anyone likely
To put a sharp knife
Into the sacred, tender vision
Of your beautiful heart.

We have a duty to befriend
Those aspects of obedience
That stand out of our house
And shout to our reason
"O please, O please,
Come out and play."

For we have not come here to take prisoners
Or to confine our wondrous spirits,

But to experience ever and ever more deeply
Our divine courage, freedom and
Light!

SEAN SUTHERLAND

And this is what breaks me into a thousand pieces I want to share

I can no longer stand to be in my apartment.
Out on the sidewalk I search the faces of those who
come towards me, ready to nod good morning.
I want more than a coffee. In the back of the 24-hour
quick mart, I see a man at the table where nobody ever sits,
unwrapping a plastic wrapped croissant.
He wears a baby blue windbreaker, with the insignia
of a bowling club. His distended eyes are splayed out
wide to each corner, unable to look at anyone directly,
which I recognize. He surveys his surroundings
as if he has just discovered nobody ever sits at his table,
beside all that toilet paper to eat their breakfast.
Whose son is he, or brother, I wonder?
Where has he gone, to be here?
We have been the same man, incapable of the quick
dignified greetings these customers share,
ordering their egg sandwiches and lottery tickets.
When he turns to me finally, and I offer him a silent hello,
he appears both curious and confused like how
someone in tears when a joke is made,
can laugh and wear half a grin.
I cannot look away, and out of my uncomfortable body
I point to his breakfast, smile, and give a thumbs up
and out of his huddled body, he raises his breakfast
three inches off the table, flakes flaking off, and with his
half-pained smile he inspires me to wear
for five blocks after, he says, "Croissant."

A Blessing

Just off the highway to Rochester, Minnesota,
Twilight bounds softly forth on the grass.
And the eyes of those two Indian ponies
Darken with kindness.
They have come gladly out of the willows
To welcome my friend and me.
We step over the barbed wire into the pasture
Where they have been grazing all day, alone.
They ripple tensely, they can hardly contain their
  happiness.
That we have come.
They bow shyly as wet swans, They love each other.
There is no loneliness like theirs.
At home once more,
They begin munching the young tufts of spring in the
  darkness.
I would like to hold the slenderer one in my arms,
For she has walked over to me
And nuzzled my left hand.
She is black and white,
Her mane falls wild on her forehead,
And the light breeze moves me to caress her long ear
That is delicate as the skin over a girl's wrist.
Suddenly I realize
That if I stepped out of my body I would break
Into blossom.

WILLIAM STAFFORD

Traveling Through the Dark

Traveling through the dark I found a deer
dead on the edge of the Wilson River road.
It is usually best to roll them into the canyon:
that road is narrow; to swerve might make more dead.

By glow of the tail-light I stumbled back of the car
and stood by the heap, a doe, a recent killing;
she had stiffened already, almost cold.
I dragged her off; she was large in the belly.

My fingers touching her side brought me the reason—
her side was warm; her fawn lay there waiting,
alive, still, never to be born.
Beside that mountain road I hesitated.

The car aimed ahead its lowered parking lights;
under the hood purred the steady engine.
I stood in the glare of the warm exhaust turning red;
around our group I could hear the wilderness listen.

I thought hard for us all—my only swerving—,
then pushed her over the edge into the river.

A Psalm Of Life. What The Heart Of The Young Man Said To The Psalmist

Tell me not, in mournful numbers,
 Life is but an empty dream!
For the soul is dead that slumbers.
 And things are not what they seem.

Life is real! Life is earnest!
 And the grave is not its goal;
Dust thou art, to dust returnest,
 Was not spoken of the soul.

Not enjoyment, and not sorrow,
 Is our destined end or way;
But to act, that each to-morrow
 Find us farther than to-day.

Art is long, and Time is fleeting,
 And our hearts, though stout and brave,
Still, like muffled drums, are beating
 Funeral marches to the grave.

In the world's broad field of battle,
 In the bivouac of Life,
Be not like dumb, driven cattle!
 Be a hero in the strife!

Trust no Future, howe'er pleasant!
 Let the dead Past bury its dead!
Act, --act in the living Present!
 Heart within, and God o'erhead!

Lives of great men all remind us
 We can make our lives sublime,

And, departing, leave behind us
  Footprints on the sands of time;--

Footprints, that perhaps another,
  Sailing o'er life's solemn main,
A forlorn and shipwrecked brother,
  Seeing, shall take heart again.

Let us, then, be up and doing,
  With a heart for any fate;
Still achieving, still pursuing,
  Learn to labor and to wait.

It Happens Like This

I was outside St. Cecelia's Rectory
smoking a cigarette when a goat appeared beside me.
It was mostly black and white, with a little reddish
brown here and there. When I started to walk away,
it followed. I was amused and delighted, but wondered
what the laws were on this kind of thing. There's
a leash law for dogs, but what about goats? People
smiled at me and admired the goat. "It's not my goat,"
I explained. "It's the town's goat. I'm just taking
my turn caring for it." "I didn't know we had a goat,"
one of them said. "I wonder when my turn is." "Soon,"
I said. "Be patient. Your time is coming." The goat
stayed by my side. It stopped when I stopped. It looked
up at me and I stared into its eyes. I felt he knew
everything essential about me. We walked on. A police-
man on his beat looked us over. "That's a mighty
fine goat you got there," he said, stopping to admire.
"It's a town's goat," I said. "His family goes back
three-hundred years with us," I said. "from the beginning."
The officer leaned forward to touch him, then stopped
and looked up at me. "Mind if I pat him?" he asked.
"Touching this goat will change your life," I said.
"It's your decision." He thought real hard for a minute,
and then stood up and said, "What's his name?" "He's
called the Prince of Peace," I said. "God! This town
is like a fairy tale. Everywhere you turn there's mystery
and wonder. And I'm just a child playing cops and robbers
forever. Please forgive me if I cry." "We forgive you,
Officer," I said. "And we understand why you, more than
anybody, should never touch the Prince." The goat and
I walked on. It was getting dark and we were beginning
to wonder where we would spend the night.

VALENCIA ROBIN

Insomnia

When the week has worn you down
to the assorted holes in your head,

all those leased words masquerading
as conversation, all your super powers

used solely for making a living, when all
that's left is the yellow blinking light of your life

half over, nothing to distract you because
it's three in the morning, no denying

the damp sheets and the tangy scent
of your day-old body as your memories

make their crash landing and you cringe
and cower, dreading their arrival. My God,

to be allowed out into the world like that,
a wounded bear disguised as a blue field,

carrying a hurt so old you thought the whole world
limped. When did you discover that knife in your heart

ran in the family, that those were history's long fingers
twisting the handle? And what dumb luck

or good ghost led you from there to here?
Do you dare to call it home? Sweet?

II. LOVE :

A strong emotion and physical sensation often felt in the heart and gut.

"Hating is easy, it is loving that is hard."

—Toni Morrison

I Give You Back

I release you, my beautiful and terrible
fear. I release you. You were my beloved
and hated twin, but now, I don't know you
as myself. I release you with all the
pain I would know at the death of
my daughters.

You are not my blood anymore.

I give you back to the white soldiers
who burned down my home, beheaded my children,
raped and sodomized my brothers and sisters.
I give you back to those who stole the
food from our plates when we were starving.

I release you, fear, because you hold
these scenes in front of me and I was born
with eyes that can never close.

I release you, fear, so you can no longer
keep me naked and frozen in the winter,
or smothered under blankets in the summer.

I release you
I release you
I release you
I release you

I am not afraid to be angry.
I am not afraid to rejoice
I am not afraid to be black.
I am not afraid to be white.
I am not afraid to be hungry.

I am not afraid to be full.
I am not afraid to be hated.
I am not afraid to be loved.

to be loved, to be loved, fear.

Oh, you have choked me, but I gave you the leash.
You have gutted me but I gave you the knife.
You have devoured me, but I laid myself across the fire.
You held my mother down and raped her,
but I gave you the heated thing.

I take myself back, fear.
You are not my shadow any longer.
I won't hold you in my hands.
You can't live in my eyes, my ears, my voice
my belly, or in my heart my heart
my heart my heart

But come here, fear
I am alive and you are so afraid
of dying.

Of Love

I have been in love more times than one,
thank the Lord. Sometimes it was lasting
whether active or not. Sometimes
it was all but ephemeral, maybe only
an afternoon, but not less real for that.
They stay in my mind, these beautiful people,
or anyway beautiful people to me, of which
there are so many. You, and you, and you,
whom I had the fortune to meet, or maybe
missed. Love, love, love, it was the
core of my life, from which, of course, comes
the word for the heart. And, oh, have I mentioned
that some of them were men and some were women
and some — now carry my revelation with you —
were trees. Or places. Or music flying above
the names of their makers. Or clouds, or the sun
which was the first, and the best, the most
loyal for certain, who looked so faithfully into
my eyes, every morning. So I imagine
such love of the world — its fervency, its shining, its
innocence and hunger to give to itself — I imagine
this is how it began.

Beannacht

For Josie

On the day when
the weight deadens
on your shoulders
and you stumble,
may the clay dance
to balance you.

And when your eyes
freeze behind
the gray window
and the ghost of loss
gets in to you,
may a flock of colors,
indigo, red, green
and azure blue
come to awaken in you
a meadow of delight.

When the canvas frays
in the curach of thought
and a stain of ocean
blackens beneath you,
may there come across the waters
a path of yellow moonlight
to bring you safely home.

May the nourishment of the earth be yours,
may the clarity of light be yours,
may the fluency of the ocean be yours,
may the protection of the ancestors be yours.

And so may a slow
wind work these words
of love around you,
an invisible cloak
to mind your life.

Sonnet XXIX

When, in disgrace with Fortune and men's eyes,
I all alone beweep my outcast state,
And trouble deaf heaven with my bootless cries,
And look upon myself, and curse my fate,
Wishing me like to one more rich in hope,
Featured like him, like him with friends possest,
Desiring this man's art and that man's scope,
With what I most enjoy contented least;
Yet in these thoughts myself almost despising —
Haply I think on thee: and then my state,
Like to the Lark at break of day arising
From sullen earth, sings hymns at Heaven's gate;
For thy sweet love rememb'red such wealth brings
That then I scorn to change my state with Kings.

ASHLEE FAYE LAMB

Love

maybe there is no leap to take,
no trek to tramp,
no endless fall to endure,
no true landing to await,
but only the making of a new choice
to be here inside this now —
wherein we are always returning
with, among, and of Love

Today

You would have loved today,
sharp winter sunshine, new windows,
too cold to take a walk.
Cardinals in the empty branches.
Eider ducks on the Sound-edge sand.
No place to go. Books
open to their final chapters. Mozart
by the fire, lighting
our endless world. The house
straightened at last.

The Owl and the Pussy Cat

I

The Owl and the Pussy-cat went to sea
In a beautiful pea-green boat
They took some honey, and plenty of money,
Wrapped up in a five-pound note.
The Owl looked up to the stars above,
And sang to a small guitar,
'O Lovely Pussy! O Pussy, my love,
What a beautiful Pussy you are,
You are,
You are!
What a beautiful Pussy you are!'

II

Pussy said to the Owl, 'You elegant fowl!
How charmingly sweet you sing!
O let us be married! too long we have tarried:
But what shall we do for a ring?'
They sailed away, for a year and a day,
To the land where the Bong-Tree grows
And there in a wood a Piggy-wig stood
With a ring at the end of his nose,
His nose,
His nose,
With a ring at the end of his nose.

III

'Dear Pig, are you willing to sell for one shilling
Your ring?' Said the Piggy, 'I will.'
So they took it away, and were married next day
By the Turkey who lives on the hill.

They dined on mince, and slices of quince,
Which they ate with a runcible spoon;
And hand in hand, on the edge of the sand,
They danced by the light of the moon,
The moon,
The moon,
They danced by the light of the moon.

You Will Hear Thunder

You will hear thunder and remember me,
And think: she wanted storms. The rim
Of the sky will be the colour of hard crimson,
And your heart, as it was then, will be on fire.

That day in Moscow, it will all come true,
when, for the last time, I take my leave,
And hasten to the heights that I have longed for,
Leaving my shadow still to be with you.

WILLIAM SHAKESPEARE

From *Romeo and Juliet*

Come, night; come, Romeo; come, thou day in night;
For thou wilt lie upon the wings of night
Whiter than new snow on a raven's back.
Come, gentle night, come, loving, black-brow'd night,
Give me my Romeo; and, when he shall die,
Take him and cut him out in little stars,
And he will make the face of heaven so fine
That all the world will be in love with night
And pay no worship to the garish sun.
O, I have bought the mansion of a love,
But not possess'd it, and, though I am sold,
Not yet enjoy'd: so tedious is this day
As is the night before some festival
To an impatient child that hath new robes
And may not wear them.

SEAN SUTHERLAND

The Unanswerable Question

My father's wedding ring encircles a little corner
of blond wood at the bottom of my sock drawer
shaped more oblong than round from all
the things he tried to shove into place:
aluminum lids to garbage cans, two-by-fours
not flush, or engine covers to outboards
that denied him all but a repair bill. Bashed down,
the ring looks up at me with the same vacuous stare
that came over him when he took a short break
from one of his fits of anger. He would look
out into the sunlight of the open basement door,
three penny nail in his mouth, or sit up
from the stern of a boat, seawater blooming
rainbows of motor oil at his feet, wrench loose
in hand, slack jawed, eyes large, as though
he had just heard a voice ask an unanswerable
question of himself. What if he were shown
a patience he never knew? I keep the drawer open
to return his stare as long as I can, not wanting
to shut it too quickly and leave him there alone.

Gratitude

I owe a great deal
to those I do not love.

The relief with which I accept
they are dearer to someone else.

The joy that it is not I
who am wolf to their sheep.

Peace unto me with them,
and freedom with them unto me,
and that is something that love cannot give
or contrive to take away.

I do not wait for them
from window to door.
Patient
almost like a sundial,
I understand
what love does not understand,
I forgive
what love would never forgive.

From meeting to letter
passes not an eternity
but merely a few days or weeks.

Travels with them are always a success,
concerts heard,
cathedrals visited,
landscapes in sharp focus.

And when we are separated

by seven mountains and rivers,
they are mountains and rivers
well known from the map.

It is thanks to them
that I live in three dimensions,
in a space non-lyrical and non-rhetorical,
with a horizon real because movable.

They themselves do not know
how much they bring in empty hands.

"I owe them nothing,"
love would say
on this open question.

Open Promise

I promise that when you forget how to smile,
I will remind you
I will place
two field hands onto
the earth of your face
and position your glowing African lips into
a crescent moon not unlike the one that
followed our true founding mothers and fathers to freedom.

I will shake away the thick coat of dust and ash
of deceit, desperation, and lies
that threatens to bury us all alive
I will fight heart to heaven combat with each painful memory
every nightmare, fear, and flash.

I will do all of this

I will carry your spirit on my shoulders,
and write sonnets to your self esteem,
walk barefoot and open souled to my death with no hesitation,
and cry out freedom songs to your dreams.

I will do all of this

Only asking for one gesture in return,
that you do the same for me.

III. FAMILY:

People related to each other by blood, marriage, circumstance or caring.

"All happy families are alike; each unhappy family is unhappy in its own way."

—Leo Tolstoy

Mother to Son

Well, son, I'll tell you:
Life for me ain't been no crystal stair.
It's had tacks in it,
And splinters,
And boards torn up,
And places with no carpet on the floor—
Bare.
But all the time
I'se been a-climbin' on,
And reachin' landin's,
And turnin' corners,
And sometimes goin' in the dark
Where there ain't been no light.
So boy, don't you turn back.
Don't you set down on the steps
'Cause you finds it's kinder hard.
Don't you fall now—
For I'se still goin', honey,
I'se still climbin',
And life for me ain't been no crystal stair.

VALENCIA ROBIN

Dutch Elm Disease

When Danny Johnson's big brother was killed in Vietnam,
Danny ran around the block five times. I counted. Ran
as if when he stopped his brother would be back in their driveway
washing his car. But nobody knew anything about time travel
back then, Star Trek hadn't even come out, Lieutenant Uhura
still on Broadway doing Blues for Mr Charlie. And even if Danny
did understand the space-time continuum, his parents
weren't having it, his mother on the porch yelling
his name, his father tackling him on the front lawn, all us kids,
the whole block standing there on pause. Which didn't exist
either. No fast forward, no reverse. We weren't even Black
yet. Was Milwaukee even Milwaukee? Is the Lincoln Park Bridge
still there, do boys like Danny still climb over the rail,
hug their bony knees to their narrow chests and plop into the river
as if there's no way his parents could lose *two* children?
Which is all I know about Vietnam, that and the way the sun hung
in the faded sky as Danny ran around and around
and held the air hostage, that and the way the thick August air
ignored the leaves of all our doomed elm trees
and let itself be held hostage. The streets were like ghosts
when they cut down those trees.

MARIE HOWE

The Boy

My older brother is walking down the sidewalk into the suburban
summer night:
white T-shirt, blue jeans — to the field at the end of the street.

Hangers Hideout the boys called it, an undeveloped plot, a pit
overgrown
with weeds, some old furniture thrown down there.

and some metal hangers clinking in the trees like wind chimes.
He's running away from home because our father wants to cut his hair.

And in two more days our father will convince me to go to him—
you know
where he is — and talk to him: No reprisals. He promised. A small
parade
of kids

in feet pajamas will accompany me, their voices like the first
peepers
in spring.
And my brother will walk ahead of us home, and my father

will shave his head bald, and my brother will not speak to anyone
the next
month, not a word, not *pass the milk*, nothing.

What happened in our house taught my brothers how to leave,
how to walk
down a sidewalk without looking back.

I was the girl. What happened taught me to follow him, whoever
he was.
calling and calling his name.

Upon Being Asked Why I Dedicated My First Book To My Mother When There's Not A Single Poem In There About Her

As Prometheus must have pocketed fire,
slipping it from Olympus in the folds
of his compassion and duplicity,
so my mother stole a Webster's pocket dictionary.
The Mansfield Jamesway Department Store
was all discounts and lighting that refused
to flatter, commerce sliding through its aisles
as my mother slipped that book into her jacket,
getting 30,000 words fatter. I know the arguments—
that's stealing; what about the owner?;
what about teaching her son what's right?
In truth, the entire Jamesway corporation
would go out of business twenty-one years later,
and I'm sure it had to do
with the Webster's Riverside Pocket Dictionary
whose pages held all the words of *Ulysses*
and *Paradise Lost* and *Look Homeward, Angel,*
but jumbled in alphabetical order.
What can I say? She stole a dictionary for me
because there were no words
a judge could use that would be worse
than her son starving
for a lexicon he could grip like a wrench
and loosen all those dumb bolts in his brain.
Receiving that dictionary taught me rectitude
and the many dictates that come down
from its cloistral mountaintop. I was suddenly rich,
a son from the most indigent family in Hampton.
How lucky — when I first started to rub against my language,
sidle up to my own tongue,
my mother stole me a book.
Years later, I gave her one back.

MARIE GABRIELE BAKER

The Ties He Wore

- light blue with a pin of the cross at his first communion
- skinny black at his wedding to Alma
- blue with gray stripes when he left for his first business trip
- silver with small white diamond stitching at this daughter's
  christening
- Paisley green-red-blue, at his parents' 50th wedding anniversary
  slung over his shoulder while arm wrestling with his cousins
- blue batik "best dad" on the afternoon of father's day
- a burgundy bowtie, when dressed as Winston Churchill for a
  costume party
- a slim, knitted tie, pea-green, for a week after cleaning out his
  father's belongings
- lilac at his daughter's wedding
  it matched her flowers

none since retirement
  except

- the skinny black one, which he uses as a belt for his gardening
  pants

Urban Youth

You'd wake me for Saturday cartoons
When you were twelve and I was two
Hong Kong Phooey, Fat Albert & the Cosby Kids.
In the '70s, everything shone bright as brass.

When you were twelve and I was two,
It was always autumn. Blue sky, flimsy clouds.
This was the '70s. Every bright day a brass
Trombone slept, leaning in your room.

Autumn-crisp air. Blue skies. Clouds
Of steam clotted the window near the stove (and
Slept in the trombone kept in your room). You
Wrote a poem about the sea and never forgot it.

Steam clotted the window near the stove
Where Mom stood sometimes staring out.
I forget now what there was to see.
So much now gone was only then beginning.

Mom stood once looking out while you and
Dad and Mike taught me to ride a two-wheeler.
So much was only then beginning. Should
I have been afraid? The hedges hummed with bees,

But it was you and Dad and Mike teaching me to ride,
Running along beside until you didn't have to hold on.
Who was afraid? The hedges thrummed with bees
That only sang. Every happy thing I've known,

You held, or ran alongside not having to hold.

CHARLES BOWE

Shoe Shine

On Sunday nights my father shined his shoes,
the business section of the Trenton Times
spread out across the kitchen table—
a tarp protecting his family's hearth from
his soles or over-eager swipes of
his rag. I'd hear the sliding closet
door first, him finding his kit of Kiwi cans:
a brown, a white (hardly touched), and a black
scooped nearly clean to its steel bottom.

Already I could hear the rhythm of
his unselfconscious breathing.
He'd been to Catholic proms during Truman,
and had to borrow black shoes from a cop.
The draft, after Korea, refused
to take him over a wrist he'd injured
while vandalizing a grocery store.

Deployed behind enemy lines in the
suburbs, he knew the importance of
black, shiny shoes. His sons entranced by
the sedative bass line of Steely Dan
while mulling the earth like Archimedes
or Appomattox as seen on a map
spread out in front of Lincoln and Grant,
he was already picturing the straight line
he'd march to Monday morning's sales calls,
the breath in his cheeks keeping time for
his black brush and buffing rag, ready
and at attention.

I Am Not My Mother

So they joke
Eventually
We all become
our mothers
Only
It's not a joke

I am not my mother

My mother grew up on a farm
In Foxholm, North Dakota
Home of foxes
And my mother
With sisters who liked gossip
And a brother who played pranks
They tipped cows for fun
Had three different sheep dogs
Named shep
And harmonized in the church choir

Her father farmed, then left for the
Post office to peddle mail most mornings
Her mother was bitter and resentful
And stuck on a farm
She taught them to sing and sew
Cook and clean
My mother learned
Etiquette, for the rare times they
Received relatives
And she was lucky to
Attend a school dance

I am not my mother

I have never milked or tipped a cow
I grew up in Detroit
Home of General Motors, Edsel Ford
Coney Dogs, Vernors
Greek Town, Motown
Corrupt Mayors and Riots
Stevie Wonder
Eminem, 8 Mile
And me

I grew up with a
Baby brother and
A black dog named
Smokey
My father left most mornings
with a badge and a gun
And then one day
He just left
My mother taught us
To clean our plates and
Play nice
I played with friends
And Barbies
We cut their hair and
Bathed them in buckets
We danced at block parties
Ate bomb pops and italian ice
And on Fridays, piled into the back
Of our neighbor's Suburban
To pick up someone else's dad
We stayed late after school
Then ate dinner for three
We played kick the can
Frisbee and freeze TV
and were called home after dark

I am not my mother

She left the farm
For the city
And was then left alone
I was left handed
And vowed never to be left
I spent my younger years
Watching my mother cry
Through a smile
I saw this as complacent
and weak
I wanted to crack her thin
Porcelain and witness
Fireworks of anger
And waterfalls of rage
To know that she had strength

I am not my mother

I moved away
Because had I stayed
Too close, she might rub off
I lived life in extremes
I saw this as strength
And then I grew up
And my mother got older
Because this is what happens

She is 70
(Don't tell her I said so)
And will live to be 100
She lives in Detroit
Alone
She shovels her own
Driveway in Michigan winters
She is a hard working

Farmers daughter
I never see her cry anymore
I never laugh more
Than when I am with her
And I know no
Stronger woman

I am not my mother

I do not have her nose
I do not believe in her God
But according to our genes
I have time to be more like her
In the rest of ways

I am not my mother

Yet

RUTH L. SCHWARTZ

The Swan in Edgewater Park

Isn't one of your prissy richpeoples' swans
Wouldn't be at home on some pristine pond
Chooses the whole stinking shoreline, candy wrappers, condoms
in its tidal fringe
Prefers to curve its muscular, slightly grubby neck
into the body of a Great Lake,
Swilling whatever it is swans swill,
Chardonnay of algae with bouquet of crud,
While Clevelanders walk by saying Look
at that big duck!
Beauty isn't the point here; of course
the swan is beautiful,
But not like Lorie at 16, when
Everything was possible—no
More like Lorie at 27
Smoking away her days off in her dirty kitchen,
Her kid with asthma watching TV,
The boyfriend who doesn't know yet she's gonna
Leave him, washing his car out back—and
He's a runty little guy, and drinks too much, and
It's not his kid anyway, but he loves her, he
Really does, he loves them both—
That's the kind of swan this is.

Last Night

We were the family
there on his bed the five of us
touching his arms, his chest,
cradling his head.

Four children
bending to
him, to ease his departure, bless
his mysterious

journey—
then I alone
uncovering the bony legs,
preparing him for rest.

Now I, in the limbo of
our fashioned earth,
cannot remember
how to be

alive,
crossing abandoned fields,
edges of cracked white sea,
high priest of sky.

The One Truth

After dreaming of radiant thrones
for sixty years, praying to a god
he never loved for strength, for mercy,
after cocking his thumbs
in the pockets of his immigrant schemes,
while he parked cars during the day
and drove a taxi all night,
after one baby was born dead
and he carved the living one's name
in windshield snow in the blizzard of 1945,
after scrubbing piss, blood,
and vomit off factory floors
from midnight to dawn,
then filling trays with peanuts,
candy, and cigarettes
in his vending machines all day,
his breath a wheezing suck
and bellowing gasp
in the fist of his chest,
after washing his face, armpits
and balls in cold back rooms,
hurrying between his hunger
for glory and his fear
of leaving nothing but debt,
after having a stroke and
falling down factory stairs,
his son screaming at him
to stop working and rest,
after being knocked down
by a blow he expected all his life,
his son begging forgiveness,
his wife crying his name,
after looking up at them

straight from hell, his soul
withering in his arms—
is this what failure is,
to end where he began,
no one but a deaf dumb God
to welcome him back,
his fits pounding at the gate—
is this the one truth,
to lie in a black pit
at the bottom of himself,
without enough breath
to say goodbye
or ask forgiveness?

three feet

wooden beds bunked and mismatched
pillow cases.
the sound of brown bottles
singing beneath,
our laughter
its own echo.

we dreamed together, i am
sure of it.
our stories carried us off into
the night. there was
safety there, there was no
fire, no listening for keys in

front doors.
we were each other's medium
brown havens.

full of questions and never
hindered by answers.
full of rich fairy tales and
soft journeys away from a hard home.

full of pink promise and
purple barrettes.

i could hear every movement
you made in your sleep.
every twist of your body,
every shake of your beads.

a resting rainbow below me.
parted by three feet.

IV. WISDOM

"The absence of delusion as revealed through insight and action."

—Dan Cayer

"Even in our sleep, pain that cannot forget falls drop by drop upon the heart, and in our own despair, against our will, comes wisdom to us by the awful grace of god."

—Aeschylus

JOY HARJO

Remember

Remember the sky that you were born under,
know each of the star's stories.
Remember the moon, know who she is. I met her
in a bar once in Iowa City.
Remember the sun's birth at dawn, that is the
strongest point of time. Remember sundown
and the giving away to night.
Remember your birth, how your mother struggled
to give you form and breath. You are evidence of
her life, and her mother's, and hers.
Remember your father. He is your life, also.
Remember the earth whose skin you are:
red earth, black earth, yellow earth, white earth
brown earth, we are earth.
Remember the plants, trees, animal life who all have their
tribes, their families, their histories, too. Talk to them,
listen to them. They are alive poems.
Remember the wind. Remember her voice. She knows the
origin of this universe. I heard her singing Kiowa war
dance songs at the corner of Fourth and Central once.
Remember that you are all people and that all people
are you.
Remember that you are this universe and that this
universe is you.
Remember that all is in motion, is growing, is you.
Remember that language comes from this.
Remember the dance that language is, that life is.
Remember.

One Cell

...contains a digitally coded database larger, in information content, than all 30 volumes of the Encyclopedia Britannica *put together.*

—Richard Dawkins, from *The Blind Watchmaker*

So in our beds or in the beds of lovers,
when we leave we leave volumes
of information, the book of our days
lost to ourselves, sloughed off into the world.
As we wander a filthy city street
we grow new cells, pungent with the old codes,
so we can stop walking, remember
the day we wept openly for a man
in a casket, the night we touched a glass
to our lips and saw all creation
in a stranger's face. The pain of childbirth
comes back, the scent of magnolia, a song
from a commercial, an afternoon carnival,
a choir. Our cells retain it, pinhead
sponges soaking up whatever we need
to keep walking, to keep stumbling into
the blinding darkness ahead.

"I Am Cherry Alive," the Little Girl Sang

For Miss Kathleen Hanlon

"I am cherry alive," the little girl sang,
"Each morning I am something new:
I am apple, I am plum, I am just as excited
As the boys who made the Hallowe'en bang:
I am tree, I am cat, I am blossom too:
When I like, if I like, I can be someone new,
Someone very old, a witch in a zoo:
I can be someone else whenever I think who,
And I want to be everything sometimes too:
And the peach has a pit and I know that too,
And I put it in along with everything
To make the grown-ups laugh whenever I sing:
And I sing: *It is true*; *It is untrue*;
I know, I know, the true is untrue,
The peach has a pit, the pit has a peach:
And both may be wrong when I sing my song,
But I don't tell the grown-ups: because it is sad,
And I want them to laugh just like I do
Because they grew up and forgot what they knew
And they are sure I will forget it some day too.
They are wrong. They are wrong. When I sang my song, I knew, I
  knew!
I am red, I am gold, I am green, I am blue,
I will always be me, I will always be new!"

For the Sleepwalkers

Tonight I want to say something wonderful
for the sleepwalkers who have so much faith
in their legs, so much faith in the invisible

arrow carved into the carpet, the worn path
that leads to the stairs instead of the window,
the gaping doorway instead of the seamless mirror.

I love the way that sleepwalkers are willing
to step out of their bodies into the night,
to raise their arms and welcome the darkness,

palming the blank spaces, touching everything.
Always they return home safely, like blind men
who know it is morning by feeling shadows.

And always they wake up as themselves again.
That's why I want to say something astonishing
like: Our hearts are leaving our bodies.

Our hearts are thirsty black handkerchiefs
flying through the trees at night, soaking up
the darkest beams of moonlight, the music

of owls, the motion of wind-torn branches.
And now our hearts are thick black fists
flying back to the glove of our chests.

We have to learn to trust our hearts like that.
We have to learn the desperate faith of sleepwalkers who rise out of their calm beds

and walk through the skin of another life.

We have to drink the stupefying cup of darkness
and wake up to ourselves, nourished and surprised.

The Star

A white star born in the evening glow
Looked to the round green world below,
And saw a pool in a wooded place
That held like a jewel her mirrored face.
She said to the pool: "Oh, wondrous deep,
I love you, I give you my light to keep.
Oh, more profound than the moving sea
That never has shown myself to me!
Oh fathomless as the sky is far,
Hold forever your tremulous star!"
But out of the woods as night grew cool
A brown pig came to the little pool;
It grunted and splashed and waded in
And the deepest place but reached its chin.
The water gurgled with tender glee
And the mud churned up in it turbidly.
The star grew pale and hid her face
In a bit of floating cloud like lace.

HOWARD NEMEROV

Trees

To be a giant and keep quiet about it,
To stay in one's own place;
To stand for the constant presence of process
And always to seem the same;
To be steady as a rock and always trembling,
Having the hard appearance of death
With the soft, fluent nature of growth,
One's Being deceptively armored,
One's Becoming deceptively vulnerable;
To be so tough, and take the light so well,
Freely providing forbidden knowledge
Of so many things about heaven and earth
For which we should otherwise have no word—
Poems or people are rarely so lovely,
And even when they have great qualities
They tend to tell you rather than exemplify
What they believe themselves to be about,
While from the moving silence of trees,
Whether in storm or calm, in leaf and naked,
Night or day, we draw conclusions of our own,
Sustaining and unnoticed as our breath,
And perilous also—though there has never been
A critical tree—about the nature of things.

Be Drunk

You have to be always drunk. That's all there is to it — it's the only way. So as not to feel the horrible burden of time that breaks your back and bends you to the earth, you have to be continually drunk.

But on what? Wine, poetry or virtue, as you wish. But be drunk.

And if sometimes, on the steps of a palace or the green grass of a ditch, in the mournful solitude of your room, you wake again, drunkenness already diminishing or gone, ask the wind, the wave, the star, the bird, the clock, everything that is flying, everything that is groaning, everything that is rolling, everything that is singing, everything that is speaking...ask what time it is and wind, wave, star, bird, clock will answer you: "It is time to be drunk! So as not to be the martyred slaves of time, be drunk, be continually drunk! On wine, on poetry or on virtue as you wish"

WENDELL BERRY

The Peace of Wild Things

When despair for the world grows in me
and I wake in the night at the least sound
in fear of what my life and my children's lives may be,
I go and lie down where the wood drake
rests in his beauty on the water, and the great heron feeds.
I come into the peace of wild things
who do not tax their lives with forethought
of grief. I come into the presence of still water.
And I feel above me the day-blind stars
waiting with their light. For a time
I rest in the grace of the world, and am free.

V. WONDER:

The fascination with the how, what, where, when and why of things.

"There are only two ways to live your life. One is as though nothing is a miracle, and the other is as though everything is a miracle."

—Albert Einstein

WILLIAM SHAKESPEARE

From *Hamlet*

To be, or not to be, that is the question:
Whether 'tis nobler in the mind to suffer
The slings and arrows of outrageous fortune,
Or to take arms against a sea of troubles
And by opposing end them. To die—to sleep,
No more; and by a sleep to say we end
The heart-ache and the thousand natural shocks
That flesh is heir to: 'tis a consummation
Devoutly to be wish'd. To die, to sleep;
To sleep, perchance to dream—ay, there's the rub:
For in that sleep of death what dreams may come,
When we have shuffled off this mortal coil,
Must give us pause—there's the respect
That makes calamity of so long life.
For who would bear the whips and scorns of time,
Th'oppressor's wrong, the proud man's contumely,
The pangs of dispriz'd love, the law's delay,
The insolence of office, and the spurns
That patient merit of th'unworthy takes,
When he himself might his quietus make
With a bare bodkin? Who would fardels bear,
To grunt and sweat under a weary life,
But that the dread of something after death,
The undiscovere'd country, from whose bourn
No traveller returns, puzzles the will,
And makes us rather bear those ills we have
Than fly to others that we know not of?
Thus conscience does make cowards of us all,
And thus the native hue of resolution
Is sicklied o'er with the pale cast of thought,
And enterprises of great pitch and moment
With this regard their currents turn awry
And lose the name of action.

Blue Bird

This morning, at the bathroom window

I strained to find the exact words

To describe the blue of a blue bird

So that even the blind could see it.

Feeling defeated as I glanced out

There...right there

A bluebird was perched on the white pergola

The only one this year,

Singing its blues

Doing all it could

To help me find the exact words.

LAURA ELIZABETH RICHARDS

Eletelephony

Once there was an elephant,
Who tried to use the telephant—
No! No! I mean an elephone
Who tried to use the telephone—
(Dear me! I am not certain quite
That even now I've got it right.)
Howe'er it was, he got his trunk
Entangled in the telephunk;
The more he tried to get it free,
The louder buzzed the telephee—
(I fear I'd better drop the song
Of elephop and telephong!)

From *Song of Myself*

Stop this day and night with me and you shall possess the origin of all poems,
You shall possess the good of the earth and sun, (there are millions of suns left,)
You shall no longer take things at second or third hand, nor look through the eyes of the dead, nor feed on the spectres in books,
You shall not look through my eyes either, nor take things from me,
You shall listen to all sides and filter them from your self.

One Cedar Tree

The cedar tree outside the window
is one
of many.
What prayers are said to it?
What voices are raised
to sacred blue sky
within its branches?
Stars
illuminate its form. The moon comes around
in a repetitious pattern,
and the sun
slopes down into a sea
that those who pray are familiar with…
(They know the tree must be the one god
because of its life they are sure.)
What do I know?
Only the prayers I send up on cedar smoke,

on sage.
Only the children who are bone-deep echoes
of a similar life.
Only the woman who sleeps generations
in my
bed.
A continuum flows like births
because somehow
the sun gallops in most mornings on the
eastern horizon.
The moon floats familiar
but changing.
And I eat, breathe, and pray to some strange god
who could be a cedar tree
outside the window.

The Negro Speaks of Rivers

(To W.E.B. DuBois)

I've known rivers:
I've known rivers ancient as the world and older than
the flow of human blood in human veins.

My soul has grown deep like the rivers.

I bathed in the Euphrates when dawns were young.
I built my hut near the Congo and it lulled me to sleep.
I looked upon the Nile and raised the pyramids above
it.
I heard the singing of the Mississippi when Abe Lincoln
went down to New Orleans, and I've seen its muddy
bosom turn all golden in the sunset.

I've known rivers:
Ancient, dusty rivers.

My soul has grown deep like the rivers.

ELIZABETH JENNINGS

A Chorus

Over the surging tides and the mountain kingdoms,
Over the pastoral valleys and the meadows,
Over the cities with their factory darkness,
Over the lands where peace is still a power,
Over all these and all this planet carries
A power broods, invisible monarch, a stranger
To some, but by many trusted. Man's a believer
Until corrupted. This huge trusted power
Is spirit. He moves in the muscle of the world,
In continual creation. He burns the tides, he shines
From the matchless skies. He is the day's surrender.
Recognize him in the eye of the angry tiger,
In the sign of a child stepping at last into sleep,
In whatever touches, graces and confesses,
In hopes fulfilled or forgotten, in promises

Kept, in the resignation of old men,
This spirit, this power, this holder together of space
Is about, is aware, is working in your breathing.
But most he is the need that shows in hunger
And in the tears shed in the lonely fastness.
And in sorrow after anger.

The Road Not Taken

Two roads diverged in a yellow wood,
And sorry I could not travel both
And be one traveler, long I stood
And looked down one as far as I could
To where it bent in the undergrowth;

Then took the other, as just as fair,
And having perhaps the better claim,
Because it was grassy and wanted wear;
Though as for that the passing there
Had worn them really about the same,

And both that morning equally lay
In leaves no step had trodden black.
Oh, I kept the first for another day!
Yet knowing how way leads on to way,
I doubted if I should ever come back.

I shall be telling this with a sigh
Somewhere ages and ages hence:
Two roads diverged in a wood, and I—
I took the one less traveled by,
And that has made all the difference.

Ambivalence

I sat in the lap of Ambivalence
Comfortable there
She resembled you mother
Fine featured and proud

And I looked down
Between my legs
At all the nascent mess below
The me that had torn
The rough strange hand
That was stitching me up
And I saw my daughter
Eyes closed to all the unaccustomed light
And I loved her
With an old and tired love
As if she had never not been there
As if it were someone I had been resisting for many years
And now
Of course
Inevitable
Here you are!
Like giving birth to my own heart
Bloody, beating and exposed now
Vulnerable in a way I had tried hard to hide
For all to see
And acting intimate with ghosts of ancestors
I had rejected, disowned and hidden in the crawl space.

I can no longer create myself
I can no longer escape
Defining truths
This moment
I am the mother now.

VI. OUTRAGE:

The inability to accept that which is unconscionable, unreasonable or unjust.

"To be a conscious human being is to often be in a state of rage and quiet sorrow."

—Anonymous

WILLIAM STAFFORD

At the Bomb Testing Site

At noon in the desert a panting lizard
waited for history, its elbows tense,
watching the curve of a particular road
as if something might happen.

It was looking at something farther off
than people could see, an important scene
acted in stone for little selves
at the flute end of consequences.

There was just a continent without much on it
under a sky that never cared less.
Ready for a change, the elbows waited.
The hands gripped hard on the desert.

GWEN NELL WESTERMAN

Dakota Homecoming

We are so honored that
        you are here, they said.
We know that this is
        your homeland, they said.
The admission price
        is five dollars, they said.
Here is your button
        for the event, they said.
It means so much to us that
        you are here, they said.
We want to write
        an apology letter, they said.
Tell us what to say.

ALLEN GINSBERG

From *"America"*

America I've given you all and now I'm nothing.
America two dollars and twentyseven cents January 17, 1956.
I can't stand my own mind.
America when will we end the human war?
Go fuck yourself with your atom bomb.
I don't feel good don't bother me.
I won't write my poem till I'm in my right mind.
America when will you be angelic?
When will you take off your clothes?
When will you look at yourself through the grave?
When will you be worthy of your million Trotskyites?
America why are your libraries full of tears?
America when will you send your eggs to India?
I'm sick of your insane demands.
When can I go into the supermarket and buy what I
    need with my good looks?
America after all it is you and I who are perfect not
    the next world.
Your machinery is too much for me.
You made me want to be a saint.
There must be some other way to settle this argument.
Burroughs is in Tangiers I don't think he'll come back
    it's sinister.
Are you being sinister or is this some form of practical
    joke?
I'm trying to come to the point.
I refuse to give up my obsession.
America stop pushing I know what I'm doing.
America the plum blossoms are falling.
I haven't read the newspapers for months, everyday
    somebody goes on trial for murder.

Grass

Pile the bodies high at Austerlitz and Waterloo,
Shovel them under and let me work —
 I am the grass; I cover all.

And pile them high at Gettysburg
And pile them high at Ypres and Verdun.
Shovel them under and let me work.
Two years, ten years, and passengers ask the conductor:
 What place is this?
 Where are we now?

 I am the grass.
 Let me work.

Beat Beat the Drums

Beat! beat! drums! — blows! bugles! blow!
Through the windows — through doors — burst like a ruthless force,
Into the solemn church, and scatter the congregation,
Into the school where the scholar is studying,
Leave not the bridegroom quiet — no happiness must he have now with
his bride,
Nor the peaceful farmer any peace, ploughing his field or gathering his grain,
So fierce you whirr and pound you drums — so shrill you bugles blow.

Beat! beat! drums! — blow! bugles! blow!
Over the traffic of cities — over the rumble of wheels in the streets;
Are beds prepared for sleepers at night in the houses? no sleepers must sleep
in those beds,
No bargainers' bargains by day — no brokers or speculators — would they
continue?
Would the talkers be talking? would the singer attempt to sing?
Would the lawyer rise in the court to state his case before the judge?
Then rattle quicker, heavier drums — you bugles wilder blow.

Beat! beat! drums! — blow! bugles! blow!
Make no parley — stop for no expostulation,
Mind not the timid — mind not the weeper or prayer,
Mind not the old man beseeching the young man,
Let not the child's voice be heard, nor the mother's entreaties,
Make even the trestles to shake the dead where they lie awaiting

the hearses,
So strong you thump O terrible drums — so loud you bugles blow.

riots

I've watched this city burn twice
in my lifetime
and the most notable event
was the reaction of the
politicians in the
aftermath
as they
proclaimed the injustice of
the system
and demanded a new
deal for the hapless and the
poor.

nothing was corrected last
time.
nothing will be changed this
time.

the poor will remain poor.
the unemployment will remain
so.
the homeless will remain
homeless

and the politicians,
fat upon the land, will thrive
forever.

the elephants of Vietnam

first they used to, he told me,
gun and bomb the elephants,
you could hear their screams over all the other sounds;
but you flew high to bomb the people,
you never saw it,
just a little flash from way up
but with the elephants
you could watch it happen
and hear how they screamed;
I'd tell my buddies, listen, you guys
stop that,
but they just laughed
as the elephants scattered
throwing up their trunks (if they weren't blown off)
opening their mouths
wide and
kicking their dumb clumsy legs
as blood ran out of big holes in their bellies.

then we'd fly back,
mission completed.
we'd get everything:
convoys, dumps, bridges, people, elephants and
all the rest.

he told me later, I
felt bad about the
elephants.

TINA CHANG

Story of Girls

Years ago, my brothers took turns holding down a girl in a room.
They weren't doing anything to her but they were laughing and
sometimes it's the laughing that does enough. They held the girl
down

for an hour and she was crying, her mouth stuffed with a small
red cloth.
Their laughing matched her crying in the same pitch. That marriage
of sound was an error and the error kept repeating itself.

There were threats of putting her in the closest or in the basement
if she didn't quiet down. One cousin told them to stop but no
one could
hear him above the high roar. After that the boy was silent,
looking down

at his hands, gesturing toward the locked door. The mother was
able
to push the door in and the boys were momentarily ashamed,
remembering
for the first time that girl was their younger sister. The
mother ran

to the girl fearful that something had been damaged. Nothing
was touched.
The brothers were merely dismissed as they jostled each other
down
the long staircase. The girl sat up to breathe a little, then a little
more.

Oftentimes it's the quiet cousin I think about.

Slavery

When first my bosom glowed with hope,
I gaz'd as from a mountain top
 On some delightful plain;
But oh! How transient was the scene —
It fled as though it had not been,
 And all my hopes were vain.

How oft this tantalizing blaze
Has led me through deception's maze;
 My friend became my foe —
Then like a plaintive dove I mourn'd,
To bitter all my sweets were turn'd,
 And tears began to flow.

Why was the dawning of my birth
Upon this vile accursed earth,
 Which is but pain to me?
Oh! that my soul had winged its flight,
When first I saw the morning light,
 To worlds of liberty!

Come melting Pity from afar
And break this vast, enormous bar
 Between a wretch and thee;
Purchase a few shorts days of time,
And bid a vassal rise sublime
 On wings of liberty.

Is it because my skin is black,
That thou should'st be so dull and slack,
 And scorn to set me free?
Then let me hasten to the grave,
The only refuge for the slave,

Who mourns for liberty.

The wicked cease from trouble there;
No more I'd languish or despair —
The weary there can rest.
Oppression's voice is heard no more,
Drudg'ry and pain, and toil are o'er.
Yes! there I shall be blest.

Freedom's Journal, 18 July 1828
Liberator, 29 March 1834

VII. LONGING:

When the heart and body ache for more.

> *"I am in this world too alone, and still*
> *not alone enough to unveil every hour."*
>
> —Rainer Maria Rilke

WILLIAM STAFFORD

Remembering

When there was air, when you could
breathe any day if you liked, and if you
wanted to you could run, I used to
climb those hills back of town and
follow a gully so my eyes were at ground
level and could look out through grass as the
  stems
bent in their tensile way, and see snow
mountains follow along, the way distance goes.

Now I carry those days in a tiny box
wherever I go. I open the lid like this
and let the light glimpse and then glance away.
There is a sigh like my breath when I do this.
Some days I do this again and again.

Piano

Softly, in the dusk, a woman is singing to me;
Taking me back down the vista of years, till I see
A child sitting under the piano, in the boom of the tingling strings
And pressing the small, poised feet of a mother who smiles as she sings.

In spite of myself, the insidious mastery of song
Betrays me back, till the heart of me weeps to belong
To the old Sunday evenings at home, with winter outside
And hymns in the cosy parlour, the tinkling piano our guide.

So now it is vain for the singer to burst into clamour
With the great black piano appassionato. The glamour
Of childish days is upon me, my manhood is cast
Down in the flood of remembrance, I weep like a child for the past.

SUSAN KINSOLVING

Sotto Voce

No one has touched me for months, maybe now it is
years. When a mere cashier touches my hand, placing change
in my palm, my heart leaps, a small sissonne of spirit.
I show a doctor where I ache and follow his eyes
until they turn into cool instruments. No one else
enjoys waiting in line, the breath of strangers nearing
the neck. But I stand waiting. I stare. And I admit
to such depravation. A plum has made me shudder
with gratitude, its soft flesh so giving, its juices
running without regard. I could not help myself. No.
I ate plums until I was sick, reaching for more. More.

I Wandered Lonely as a Cloud

I wandered lonely as a cloud
That floats on high o'er vales and hills,
When all at once I saw a crowd,
A host, of golden daffodils;
Beside the lake, beneath the trees,
Fluttering and dancing in the breeze.

Continuous as the stars that shine
And twinkle on the milky way,
They stretch in never-ending line
Along the margin of a bay:
Ten thousand saw I at a glance,
Tossing their heads in sprightly dance.

The waves beside them danced; but they
Out-did the sparkling waves in glee:
A poet could not but be gay,
In such a jocund company:
I gazed—and gazed—but little thought
What wealth the show to me had brought:

For oft, when on my couch I lie
In vacant or in pensive mood,
They flash upon that inward eye
Which is the bliss of solitude;
And then my heart with pleasure fills,
And dances with the daffodils.

W.B. YEATS

The Lake Isle of Innisfree

I will arise and go now, and go to Innisfree,
And a small cabin build there, of clay and wattles made:
Nine bean-rows will I have there, a hive for the honey-bee;
And live alone in the bee-loud glade.

And I shall have some peace there, for peace comes dropping
slow,
Dropping from the veils of the morning to where the cricket
sings;
There midnight's all a glimmer, and noon a purple glow,
And evening full of linnet's wings.

I will arise and go now, for always night and day
I hear lake water lapping with low sounds by the shore;
While I stand on the roadway, or on the pavements grey,
I hear it in the deep heart's core.

A Shropshire Lad 2: Loveliest of trees, the cherry now

Loveliest of trees, the cherry now
Is hung with bloom along the bough,
And stands about the woodland ride
Wearing white for Eastertide.

Now, of my threescore years and ten,
Twenty will not come again,
And take from seventy springs a score,
It only leaves me fifty more.

And since to look at things in bloom
Fifty springs are little room,
About the woodlands I will go
To see the cherry hung with snow.

To a Stranger

Passing stranger! you do not know how longingly I look upon you,
You must be he I was seeking or she I was seeking, (it comes to me, as of a dream,)
I have somewhere surely lived a life of joy with you,
All is recall'd as we flit by each other, fluid, affectionate, chaste, matured,
You grew up with me, were a boy with me, or a girl with me,
I ate with you, and slept with you, your body has become not yours only, nor left my body mine only,
You give me the pleasure of your eyes, face, flesh, as we pass, you take of my beard, breast, hands, in return,
I am not to speak to you, I am to think of you when I sit alone, or wake at night alone,
I am to wait, I do not doubt I am to meet you again,
I am to see to it that I do not lose you.

I Don't Know If You're Alive or Dead

I don't know if you're alive or dead.
Can you on earth be sought,
Or only when the sunsets fade
Be mourned serenely in my thought?

All is for you: the daily prayer,
The sleepless heat at night,
And of my verses, the white
Flock, and of my eyes, the blue fire.

No-one was more cherished, no-one tortured
Me more, not
Even the one who betrayed me to torture,
Not even the one who caressed me and forgot.

Sunbeam

I pray to the sunbeam from the window -
It is pale, thin, straight.
Since morning I have been silent,
And my heart - is split.
The copper on my washstand
Has turned green,
But the sunbeam plays on it
So charmingly.
How Innocent it is, and simple,
In the evening calm,
But to me in this deserted temple
It's like a golden celebration,
And a consolation.

Fitting in

1

Today's work outfit is especially a costume,
the gray wool pencil skirt
made for a boy's body, the turquoise sleeveless blouse
that's my uniform under cardigans
it boasts washable, drip dry convenience,
it all says "I'm going to work, I work,"
like no other outfit I own, except maybe the
black shift dress that is my third LBD, that gets worn
for special lectures and monthly administrative leadership
meetings important to be seen at, as if one more or less
manager is visible in the auditorium,
in this disintegrating seat.

2

I rounded the curve of the yellow cinderblock
walls of Highland View Elementary School,
the year before I got glasses, before my brother's birth,
I walk along the school hallway
at a quiet moment when everyone
else is in class, moving
at my own pokey pace. I wonder how my arms
were supposed to move, and a teacher caught me
trying different swings –
with my steps,
against my steps, then
flapping them
in a way that must have looked odd,
and I flew outside myself, first saw
what others might see, became self conscious,
a feeling that has not left me yet.

A Summer Day By The Sea

The sun is set; and in his latest beams
Yon little cloud of ashen gray and gold,
Slowly upon the amber air unrolled,
The falling mantle of the Prophet seems.
From the dim headlands many a lighthouse gleams,
The street-lamps of the ocean; and behold,
O'erhead the banners of the night unfold;
The day hath passed into the land of dreams.
O summer day beside the joyous sea!
O summer day so wonderful and white,
So full of gladness and so full of pain!
Forever and forever shalt thou be
To some the gravestone of a dead delight,
To some the landmark of a new domain.

Stopping By Woods On A Snowy Evening

Whose woods these are I think I know.
His house is in the village, though;
He will not see me stopping here
To watch his woods fill up with snow.

My little horse must think it's queer
To stop without a farmhouse near
Between the woods and frozen lake
The darkest evening of the year.

He gives his harness bells a shake
To ask if there's some mistake.
The only other sound's the sweep
Of easy wind and downy flake.

The woods are lovely, dark, and deep,
But I have promises to keep,
And miles to go before I sleep,
And miles to go before I sleep.

Birches

When I see birches bend to left and right
Across the lines of straighter darker trees,
I like to think some boy's been swinging them.
But swinging doesn't bend them down to stay.
Ice-storms do that. Often you must have seen them
Loaded with ice a sunny winter morning
After a rain. They click upon themselves
As the breeze rises, and turn many-colored
As the stir cracks and crazes their enamel.
Soon the sun's warmth makes them shed crystal shells
Shattering and avalanching on the snow-crust,
Such heaps of broken glass to sweep away
You'd think the inner dome of heaven had fallen.
They are dragged to the withered bracken by the load,
And they seem not to break; though once they are bowed
So low for long, they never right themselves:
You may see their trunks arching in the woods
Years afterwards, trailing their leaves on the ground
Like girls on hands and knees that throw their hair
Before them over their heads to dry in the sun.
But I was going to say when Truth broke in
With all her matter-of-fact about the ice-storm
(Now am I free to be poetical?)
I should prefer to have some boy bend them
As he went out and in to fetch the cows,
Some boy too far from town to learn baseball,
Whose only play was what he found himself,
Summer or winter, and could play alone.
One by one he subdued his father's trees
By riding them down over and over again
Until he took the stiffness out of them,
And not one but hung limp, not one was left
For him to conquer. He learned all there was

To learn about not launching out too soon
And so not carrying the tree away
Clear to the ground. He always kept his poise
To the top branches, climbing carefully
With the same pains you use to fill a cup
Up to the brim, and even above the brim.
Then he flung outward, feet first, with a swish,
Kicking his way down through the air to the ground.
So was I once myself a swinger of birches.
And so I dream of going back to be.
It's when I'm weary of considerations,
And life is too much like a pathless wood
Where your face burns and tickles with cobwebs
Broken across it, and one eye is weeping
From a twig's having lashed across it open.
I'd like to get away from earth awhile
And then come back to it and begin over.
May no fate willfully misunderstand me
And half grant what I wish and snatch me away
Not to return. Earth's the right place for love:
I don't know where it's likely to go better.
I'd like to go by climbing a birch tree,
And climb black branches up a snow-white trunk
Toward heaven, till the tree could bear no more,
But dipped its top and set me down again.
That would be good both going and coming back.
One could do worse than be a swinger of birches.

VIII. DEATH:

When the breathing stops.

"When I learned I would be dead in a year, I learned to live. "

—Richard Gambe

MARY OLIVER

When Death Comes

When death comes
like the hungry bear in autumn;
when death comes and takes all the bright coins from his purse
to buy me, and snaps the purse shut;
when death comes
like the measle-pox
when death comes
like an iceberg between the shoulder blades,
I want to step through the door full of curiosity, wondering:
what is it going to be like, that cottage of darkness?
And therefore I look upon everything
as a brotherhood and a sisterhood,
and I look upon time as no more than an idea,
and I consider eternity as another possibility,
and I think of each life as a flower, as common
as a field daisy, and as singular,
and each name a comfortable music in the mouth,
tending, as all music does, toward silence,
and each body a lion courage, and something
precious to the earth.

When it's over, I want to say all my life
I was a bride married to amazement.
I was the bridegroom, taking the world into my arms.
When it's over, I don't want to wonder
if I have made of my life something particular, and real.
I don't want to find myself sighing and frightened,
or full of argument.
I don't want to end up simply having visited this world.

The Long Boat

When his boat snapped loose
from its mooring, under
the screaking of the gulls,
he tried at first to wave
to his dear ones on shore,
but in the rolling fog
they had already lost their faces.
Too tired even to choose
between jumping and calling,
somehow he felt absolved and free
of his burdens, those mottoes
stamped on his name-tag:
conscience, ambition, and all
that caring.
He was content to lie down
with the family ghosts
in the slop of his cradle,
buffeted by the storm,
endlessly drifting.
Peace! Peace!
To be rocked by the Infinite!
As if it didn't matter
which way was home;
as if he didn't know
he loved the earth so much
he wanted to stay forever.

MARIE HOWE

The Last Time

The last time we had dinner together in a restaurant
with white tablecloths, he leaned forward

and took my two hands in his hands and said,
I'm going to die soon. I want you to know that.

And I said, I think I do know.
And he said, What surprises me is that you don't.

And I said, I do. And he said, What?
And I said, Know that you're going to die.

And he said, No, I mean know that you are.

Mourners

After the funeral, the mourners gather
under the rustling churchyard maples
and talk softly, like clusters of leaves.
White shirt cuffs and collars flash in the shade:
highlights on deep green water.
They came this afternoon to say goodbye,
but now they keep saying hello and hello,
peering into each other's faces,
slow to let go of each other's hands.

MARY ELIZABETH FRYE

Do Not Stand at My Grave and Weep

Do not stand at my grave and weep,
I am not there, I do not sleep.
I am in a thousand winds that blow,
I am the softly falling snow.
I am the gentle showers of rain,
I am the fields of ripening grain.
I am in the morning hush,
I am in the graceful rush
Of beautiful birds in circling flight,
I am the starshine of the night.
I am in the flowers that bloom,
I am in a quiet room.
I am in the birds that sing,
I am in each lovely thing.
Do not stand at my grave and cry,
I am not there. I do not die.

For the Anniversary of My Death

Every year without knowing it I have passed the day
When the last fires will wave to me
And the silence will set out
Tireless traveller
Like the beam of a lightless star

Then I will no longer
Find myself in life as in a strange garment
Surprised at the earth
And the love of one woman
And the shamelessness of men
As today writing after three days of rain
Hearing the wren sing and the falling cease
And bowing not knowing to what

When I Have Fears That I May Cease to Be

When I have fears that I may cease to be
Before my pen has gleaned my teeming brain,
Before high-pilèd books, in charactery,
Hold like rich garners the full ripened grain;
When I behold, upon the night's starred face.
Huge cloudy symbols of a high romance,
And think that I may never live to trace
Their shadows with the magic hand of chance;
And when I feel, fair creature of an hour,
That I shall never look upon thee more,
Never have relish in the faery power
Of unreflecting love — then on the shore
Of the wide world I stand alone, and think
Till love and fame to nothingness do sink.

Worthington State Forest

For comfort we go to the one place death
takes off her mask, where lichens
and mushrooms can turn a trunk of a dead
sapling into a decorative staff
you'd hold while telling a story about
the unexpected shortness of life,
where death smells good, and we look at
a struggling birch without opinion
or preference about its survival.
where fractured limbs hang from bodies.
no one rushing to set them in a cast,
no cursing the traffic on the way to
the hospital, no nosy neighbors,
lasagna in hand, asking how they
can help and whispering how that boy
is never careful, that mother can't
control him. Logs twenty or thirty
years old know how to keep the shape of
a living trunk, and rotting from the inside
is feeding a creature whose name we can
sometimes remember. Where death gets thanked
for freezing a moment in time,
applauded for her comments, abstract
and on point, about the living.

Burying Father

In Seaside Heights, NJ, my father would shade us
with his huge beer belly that curved down
over the copper snap of his red cut-offs.
My brother and I found refuge from the sun there,
beneath the frame that was a delight to bury.
He stood over us for the length of digging,
positioning so his shadow would shelter us.
The surface sand was easiest, ran through our hands
quicker than dimes as the ocean registered
the latest items of its ancient complaint. Then
the lower soil, compact, years of compression
(what did we know of compression?), harder
to get through, pull up, finally discard. We knew our father
wouldn't fit in any shallow ditch—too immense
for that easy burial — and so in the darkness we pushed.
Back then I hadn't read much but I had read about treasures
in Boy's Life, all sorts of value too deep for detectors,
covered by years of tidal shifts and wind's constant backhoe.
We never found anything. How I miss those days now —
in 25 years, my brother and I would be friends
who hardly speak, but in those days we'd shovel together,
doing our best to bury Dad. How we enjoyed his shadow —
a good darkness then — never thinking about the unhealthiness
of such an imposing frame, or anything as grave.

I Was Afraid Of Dying

Once,
I was afraid of dying
In a field of dry weeds.
But now,
All day long I have been walking among damp fields,
Trying to keep still, listening
To insects that move patiently.
Perhaps they are sampling the fresh dew that gathers slowly
In empty snail shells
And in the secret shelters of sparrow feathers fallen on the
earth.

WALT WHITMAN

From *"Song of Myself"*

The spotted hawk swoops by and accuses me, he com-
plains of my gab and my loitering.

I too am not a bit tamed, I too am untranslatable,
I sound my barbaric yawp over the roofs of the world.

The last scud of day holds back for me,
It flings my likeness after the rest and true as any on the
shadow'd wilds,
It coaxes me to the vapor and the dusk.

I depart as air, I shake my white locks at the runaway sun,
I effuse my flesh in eddies, and drift it in lacy jags.

I bequeath myself to the dirt to grow from the grass I love,
If you want me again look for me under your boot-soles.

You will hardly know who I am or what I mean,
But I shall be good health to you nevertheless,
And filter and fibre your blood.

Failing to fetch me at first keep encouraged,
Missing me one place search another,
I stop somewhere waiting for you.

Aeschylus was a great classical Greek dramatist. 524-456 BC

Anna Akhmatova was one of the most prolific and significant Russian poets of the 20th century. 1889-1966

Maria Gabriele Baker is a writer of plays, poetry and prose as well as a translator and educator. She is a professor of writing and teaches at Pratt University. She lives in Brooklyn, NY.

James Baldwin was an American novelist, playwright and human rights activist from Harlem, New York. *Notes of A Native Son, The Fire Next Time*, and *If Beale Street Could Talk* are among his enormous body of work. He is considered by many to be one the top 100 great American writers of the 20th century.1924-1987

Coleman Barks is an American poet and interpreter of mystic writings, including the popular thirteenth century Persian Poet, Rumi.

Wendell Berry is an American poet, teacher, writer of essays, short stories, novels and also is farmer from Kentucky.

Charles Bowe is a poet and screen writer. He lives in the Hudson Valley, New York.

Charles Bukowski was a German/American poet, novelist and short story writer. 1920-1994

Tina Chang is an American poet, editor and educator. In 2010 she was named Poet Laureate of Brooklyn, New York.

Dan Cayer is a Buddhist teacher and Alexander instructor. He lives with his family in the Hudson Valley, New York.

Lucille Clifton was an American poet, writer and educator. From 1975-1985 she was the Poet Laureate of Maryland. 1936-2010.

Emily Dickinson was an American poet from Amherst, Mass. She was known as a recluse and is recognized posthumously for her style, form and syntax, regarded by many as one of the great poets of the 19th century. 1830-1886

Albert Einstein was a German born theoretical physicist, educator and writer who developed the theory of relativity. 1879-1955.

Mary Elizabeth Frye was an American poet and florist. 1905-2004

Robert Frost was an extremely prolific and popular American poet who received four separate Pulitzer Prizes in Poetry; in 1924 for *New Hampshire: a poem with notes and grace notes*, 1931 for *Collected Poems*, 1937 for *A Further Range* and in 1943 for *A Witness Tree.* 1874-1963

Richard Gambe was as an actor and a beloved soldier for empathy. He lived and died in NYC 1950-1989

Jack Gilbert was an American novelist, writer and poet who wrote nine volumes of poetry.1925-2012

Allen Ginsberg was an American poet, philosopher and driving force of the Beat Generation. His poem *Howl*, stunned the literary world. 1926-1997

Johann Wolfgang von Goethe was a highly esteemed German born poet, playwright, novelist, theater director and critic. 1749-1832

Salisa Lynn Grant is an American poet and educator raised in Duluth, Minnesota. She is currently completing her Ph.D. in African-American Literature at Howard University and lives in Washington DC. *These Black Hands* is her debut collection of poetry

Uta Hagen was an American actress, teacher, poet and writer. She and her husband Herbert Berghof established the landmark HB Studios in Greenwich Village, NY. She authored two invaluable books on acting, *Respect for Acting* and *Challenge To The Actor*. 1919-2004

Joy Harjo is an American poet, musician and author. She recently became the first Native American United States Poet Laureate.

Andrea Hines is a poet and writer living in Brooklyn, NY. She teaches writing at The Writers Studio, where she studied from 2015-2018.

Edward Hirsch is an American poet and critic, and author of nine volumes of poetry. He has received many awards for his contribution to literature as well as the Guggenheim Fellowship in 1985 and a five year MacArthur Fellowship in 1997.

George M.Horton was an American poet and one of the first poets to have his work published while enslaved in North Carolina on a tobacco plantation. In 1996 he was inducted into the North Carolina Hall of Fame. 1798-1884

A.E. Housman was an English classical scholar, educator and poet. 1859-1936

Marie Howe is an American poet. In 2012 she was named The State Poet for New York. She has received a Guggenheim and National Endowment for the Arts Fellowship. She teaches at Sarah Lawrence College.

Langston Hughes was an American poet, social activist, novelist, playwright and columnist from Joplin, Missouri. While he traveled extensively, Harlem NY was his primary home. 1902-1967

Elizabeth Jennings was an English poet of plain spoken, traditional verse. 1926-2001

Franz Kafka was a German speaking Bohemian novelist and short story writer. While quite prolific, he is famous for his book *Metamorphosis*. 1883-1924

John Keats was an English Romantic poet. Although he died at age 25, he had a remarkable career as a poet. 1795-1821

Susan Kinsolving is widely published in numerous anthologies and reviews, and has authored three volumes of poetry.

Ted Kooser is an American poet. He is the author of 12 collections of poetry, winning the Pulitzer Prize for Poetry in 2005 for his collection *Delights and Shadows*.

Stanley Kunitz was a prolific American poet. He was given numerous awards for his contribution to poetry and was the tenth Poet Laureate of the United States in 2000. 1905-2006

Daniel Ladinsky is an American poet and translator of mystical poetry, including The Gift by the Persian poet Hafiz.

Ashlee Faye Lamb is an American freelance wildcraft artist and poet. She lives in Chicago, Illinois.

Dorianne Laux is an American poet. She has authored 24 volumes of poetry and is published in numerous poetry reviews.

D H Lawrence was an English novelist and poet. 1885-1930

Edward Lear was an American artist, musician and poet. 1812-1888

Henry Wadsworth Longfellow was a popular nineteenth century American poet and educator. 1807-1882

Toni Morrison was a prolific American writer, editor, poet, educator and activist. She received the Pulitzer Prize in 1988 for her novel *Beloved* and the Nobel Prize for Literature in 1993. 1931- 2019.

W S Merwin was an American poet, novelist and translator. He was awarded two Pulitzer Prizes, in 1971 for *The Carrier of Ladders* and again in 2009 for *The Shadow of Sirius* as well as the National Book Award for Poetry for *Migration: New and Selected Poems* in 2005. 1927-2019

Bill Moyers is an American journalist, writer and political commentator. His book *The Language of Life* is a massive celebration of poets and their work.

Alexandra Napier is an actor and writer living in New York City. She is working on a debut poetry collection, *Emotional Acrostics.*

Howard Nemerov was an American poet, twice awarded United States Poet Laureate. In 1997 he won the National Book Award for Poetry, Pulitzer Prize for Poetry and Bollingen Award for his book, *Collected Poems.* 1920-1991

Pablo Neruda was a Chilean poet, diplomat, and politician. *Twenty Love Poems and A Song of Despair* is his internationally famous collection of passionate poetry. He won the Nobel Prize for Literature in 1971. 1904-1973

Mary Oliver was a prolific American writer, poet and essayist. In 1984 she was awarded the Pulitzer Prize for *American Primitive* and 1992 she received the National Book Award for her collection *New and Selected Poems.* 1935-2019

John O'Donohue was an Irish poet, author, scholar and philosopher. He traveled the world reading his work and lecturing on the spiritual landscape of the Irish imagination. *Anam Cara* is among his many revered books.1956-2008

Laura Elizabeth Richards was an American poet, writer and biographer. She was born in Boston Mass. 1850-1943

Rainer Maria Rilke was a Bohemian poet, essayist and novelist, recognized by many as a master of verse. *The Duino Elegies* and *Letters to A Young Poet* are considered by many to be his greatest works. His work remains extremely popular and widely read in America and around the world.1875-1926

Valencia Robin is an American poet and visual artist. Her poems have been published in numerous literary magazines. *Ridiculous Light* is her debut collection.

Carl Sandberg was an American poet, biographer and editor, and awarded two Pulitzer Prizes in Poetry. He was a human rights activist and the first white man to be honored by the NAACP as a major prophet in the civil rights movement. 1878-1967

Danielle Savin is an American poet, yoga instructor and proprietor of two bars called Bob's Your Uncle. She divides her time between New York City and Miami, Florida.

Philip Schultz is an American poet and founder of The Writers Studio in New York City. He was awarded the 2008 Pulitzer Prize in Poetry.

Ruth L. Schwartz is an American poet. She lives in the San Francisco Bay area.

Delmore Schwartz was an American poet and short story writer. He authored 14 published works both while he was alive and posthumously. 1913-1966

William Shakespeare was born in England and remains the most prolific playwright and poet of all time. 1564-1616

Suzanne Shepherd is an actress, director and poet. She divides her time between Ghent and New York City, New York.

Tracy K. Smith is an American poet, writer and educator. She was the Poet Laureate of the United States from 2017-2019 and was awarded the Pulitzer prize for her poetry collection *Life on Mars*.

William Stafford was an American poet, writer and pacifist. He received the National Book Award in 1963 and was the United States Poet Laureate in 1970. 1914-1993

Rose Styron is an American poet, translator, journalist and human rights activist. She has served on the boards of Amnesty International. PEN, and the Robert F. Kennedy Foundation. She has published several books of poetry. She lives on Martha's Vineyard, Mass.

Sean Sutherland is an American poet. He has had poems published in several literary magazines including Sleet magazine, and The Maine Review for which he won honorable mention in 2015. He was nominated for Pushcart Prize, and he studies with Philip Schultz in his master class at the Writers Studio in NYC.

Wislawa Szymborska was a Polish poet, writer and translator. She was awarded the Noble Prize in Literature in 1996 for her contribution of poetry. 1923-2012

James Tate was an American poet. In 1991 he received the Pulitzer Prize for his collection, *Selected Poems* and in 1994 he was awarded the National Book Award for Poetry for his volume *Worshipful Company of Fletchers.* 1943-2015

Sara Teasdale was an American lyric poet. 1884-1933

Leo Tolstoy was a Russian novelist, considered to be one of the greatest writers of all time. *Anna Karenina* and *War and Peace* are among his masterpieces. 1828-1910

B J Ward is an American poet, writer and educator. He lives in New Jersey.

Walt Whitman was an American poet, essayist, and journalist. *Leaves of Grass* is his timeless and popular collection of poetry. He is known by many to be "America's poet."1819-1892

Gwen Nell Westerman is a Dakota educator, writer, artist, activist and poet. She is the director of the Native American Literary Symposium and a citizen of the Cherokee Nation through her mother.

David Whyte is an internationally acclaimed American poet. He travels worldwide lecturing, and reading his vast body of work and the poetry of others to large audiences. He makes his home in the Pacific Northwest.

William Wordsworth was an English Romantic poet who along with Samuel Taylor Coleridge helped launch the the Romantic Age of English literature. 1770-1850

William Butler Yeats was an Irish poet and one of the foremost figures of twentieth century literature. He helped found the Abby Theater in Dublin, Ireland and was awarded the Nobel Prize in Literature in 1923. 1865-1939

PERMISSION ACKNOWLEDGEMENTS

Anna Akhmatova "I Don't Know," "Sunbeam," "You Will Hear Thunder" Public Domain.

Maria Gabriel Baker "The Ties He Wore" by permission of author; translation of all excerpts from Rilke's poetry by permission of translator.

Coleman Barks "The Guest House" from RUMI: THE BOOK OF LOVE: POEMS OF EXTACY AND LONGING, TRANSLATIONS AND COMMENTARY by COLEMAN BARKS ET AL. Copyright © 2003 by Coleman Barks. Reprinted by permission of HarperCollins Publishers.

Charles Baudelaire "Be Drunk" Public Domain.

Wendell Berry "The Peace of Wild Places" Copyright © 2012 by Wendell Berry. From NEW COLLECTED POEMS. Reprinted by permission of Counterpoint Press.

Charles Bowe "Shoe Shine," Worthington State Forest by permission of author.

Charles Bukowski "the elephants of Vietnam" from PLEASURES OF THE DAMNED by Charles Bukowski. Copyright © 2007 By Linda Lee Bukowski. Reprinted by permission of Harper Collins Publishers.

"Riots" from THE PLEASURES OF THE DAMNED by CHARLES BUKOWSKI. COPYRIGHT © 2007 By Linda Lee Bukowski. Reprinted by permission of HarperCollins Publishers.

Tina Chang "Story of Girls" from *Of Gods and Strangers.* Copyright © 2011 by Tina Chang.

Reprinted with permission of The Permissions Company, LLC on behalf of Four Way Books, www.fourwaybooks.com.

Robert Frost "Stopping By The Woods On A Snowy Evening," "Birches,""The Road Not Taken," Public Domain.

Mary Elizabeth Frye "DO NOT STAND AT MY GRAVE" Public Domain.

Jack Gilbert "Failing and Flying" from COLLECTED POEMS by Jack Gilbert, copyright © 2012 by Jack Gilbert. Used by permission of Alfred A. Knopf, an imprint of the Knopf Doubleday Publishing Group, a division of Penguin Random House LLC. All rights reserved.

Allen Ginsberg Excerpt of 32 lines from "AMERICA" FROM COLLECTED POEMS 1947-1980 byAllen Ginsberg. Copyright © 1956,1959 by Allen Ginsberg. Reprinted by permission of HarperCollins Publishers.

Salisa Lynn Grant "three feet" and "Open Promise" by permission of author from her book THESE BLACK HANDS.

Joy Harjo "I Give You Back." Copyright © 1983 by Joy Harjo. "One Cedar Tree." Copyright © 1983 by Joy Harjo. "Remember." Copyright © 1983 by Joy Harjo, from SHE HAD SOME HORSES by Joy Harjo. Used by permission of W.W. Norton & Company. Inc.

Andrea Hines "Fitting In" by permission of author.

Edward Hirsch "For The Sleepwalkers" from FOR THE SLEEPWALKERS by Edward Hirsch, copyright © 1981by Edward Hirsch. Used by permission Alfred A Knopf, an imprint the Knopf Doubleday Publishing Group, a division of Penguin Random House LLC. All rights reserved.

Marie Howe "The Boy," "The Last Time," from WHAT THE LIVING DO by Marie Howe. Copyright © 1997 by Marie Howe. Used by permission of W W Norton & Company. Inc.

George M.Horton "Slavery" Public Domain.

A.E. Housman "A Shropshire Lad." Public Domain.

Langston Hughes "Mother to Son" and " The Negro Speaks of Rivers" from THE COLLECTED POEMS OF LANGSTON HUGHES by Langston Hughes, edited by Arnold Rampersad with David Roessel, Associate Editor, copyright © 1984 by the Estate of Langston Hughes. Used by permission of Alfred A. Knopf, an imprint of the Knopf Doubleday Publishing Group, a division pf Penguin Random HouseLLC. All rights reserved.

Elizabeth Jennings "A Chorus" Public Domain.

John Keats "When I Have Fears That I Shall Cease To Be" Public Domain.

Susan Kinsolving "Sotto Voce," From DAILIES AND RUSHES, copyright © 1999 by Susan Kinsolving. By permission of Grove/Atlantic Inc.

Ted Kooser, "Mourners" from *Delights & Shadows.* Copyright © 2004 by Ted Kooser. Reprinted with permission of The Permissions Company, LLC on behalf of Copper Canyon Press, www.coppercanyonpress.org.

Stanley Kunitz "The Layers" Copyright © 1978 by Stanley Kunitz, "The Long Boat." Copyright © 1985 by Stanley Kunitz, from THE COLLECTED POEMS by Stanley Kunitz. Used by permission of W W Norton & Company, Inc.

Daniel Ladinsky "We Are Not Here To Take Prisoners." From the Penguin Publication, The Gift, Poems by Hafiz. Copyright 1999 and used with his permission.

Ashlee Lamb "Love" used by the author's permission.

Dorianne Laux "One Cell," from FACTS ABOUT THE MOON by Dorianne Laux. Copyright © 2006 by Dorianne Laux. Used by permission of W W Norton & Company, Inc.

D H Lawrence "Piano" Public Domain.

Edward Lear "The Owl and The Pussy Cat" Public Domain.

Henry Wadsworth Longfellow "O Psalm of Life," "Summer by The Sea," Public Domain.

W.S. Merwin, "For The Anniversary of My Death" from *The Essential W.S.Merwin,* edited by Michael Wiegers. Copyright © 1967 by W.S. Merwin. Reprinted with permission of The Permissions Company LLC on behalf of Copper Canyon Press. www.coppercanyonpress.org.

Alexandra Napier "Ambivalence" by permission of author.

Howard Nemerov "Trees" from THE COLLECTED POEMS of Howard Nemerov by permission of Alexander Nemerov.

John O'Donohue "Beannacht" for Josie from ANAM CARA: A BOOK OF CELTIC WISDOM by JOHN O'DONOHUE. Copyright © 1997by John O'Donohue. Reprinted by permission of Harper Collins Publishers.

Mary Oliver - OF LOVE from *Red Bird* by Mary Oliver- published by Beacon Press, Boston; Copyright © 2008 by Mary Oliver. WHEN DEATH COMES- from *New and Selected Poems* by Mary Oliver-published by Beacon Press, Boston. Copyright © 1992 by Mary Oliver.Reprinted by permission of The Charlotte Sheedy Literary Agency Inc.

Rainer Maria Rilke excerpts from THE DUINO ELEGIES -translated from the German by Maria Gabriele Baker. by permission of translator.

Laura Elizabeth Richards "Eletelephony" Public Domain.

Valencia Robin "Dutch Elm Disease" and "Insomnia" from RIDICULOUS LIGHT. Copyright © 2019 by Valencia Robin. Reprinted with the permission of Persea Books, Inc. (New York), www.perseabooks.com. All rights reserved.

Carl Sandburg "Grass," Public Domain.

Danielle Savin "I Am Not My Mother" by permission of author.

Philip Schultz "The One Truth" from FAILURE: Poems by Philip Schultz. Copyright © 2007 by Philip Schultz. Reprinted by permission of Houghton Mifflin Harcourt Publishing Company. all rights reserved.

Delmore Schwartz "I Am Cherry Alive, the Little Girl Sang" by Delmore Schwartz, from SELECTED POEMS, copyright © 1959 by Delmore Schwartz. Reprinted by New Directions Publishing Corp.

Ruth L. Schwartz "The Swan at Edgewater Park" from EDGEWATER PARK by Ruth L. Schwartz. Copyright © 2002 by Ruth L.Schwartz. Used by permission of HarperCollins Publishers.

William Shakespeare; Sonnets LX, XXIX and excerpt from Romeo and Juliet and excerpt from Hamlet. Public Domain.

Suzanne Shepherd "Blue Bird" by permission of author.

Tracy K. Smith "Urban Youth" and "Beatific" from WADE IN THE WATER. Copyright © 2018 by Tracy K. Smith. Reprinted with permission of The Permissions Company, LLC on behalf of Greywolf Press, Minneapolis, Minnesota, www.graywolfpress.org.

William Stafford, "Traveling Through the Dark," "At the Bomb Testing Site" and "Remembering" from *The Way It Is: New and Selected Poems.* Copyright © 1960, 1962, 1982, 1998 by William Stafford and the Estate of William Stafford. reprinted with the permission of The Permissions Company, LLC on behalf of Greywolf Press, Minneapolis, Minnesota, www.greywolfpress.org.

Rose Styron "Last Night" and "Today" by permission of author.

Sean Sutherland "The Unanswerable Question" and "And This Is What Breaks Me Into A Thousand Pieces I Want To Share" by permission of the author.

Wislawa Szymborska "Gratitude" from Sounds, Feelings and Thoughts: seventy poems. Published by Princeton University Press. Copyright © 1981. Permission to print by Copyright Clearance Center.

James Tate "IT HAPPENED LIKE THIS" Copyright © 2003 permission to print by Dara Wier. copyright owner/agent.

Sara Teasdale "The Star" Public Domain.

B J Ward "Upon Being Asked Why I Dedicated My First Book To My Mother When There Is Not A Single Poem In There About Her" and " Burying Father" from *Gravedigger's Birthday,* by B J Ward, published by North Atlantic Books. Copyright © 2002 by B J Ward. Reprinted by permission of the publisher.

Gwen Nell Westerman "Dakota Homecoming" by permission of author. "Dakota Homecoming" was published in *New Poets of Native Nations,* Ed. Heid E. Erdrich. Minneapolis: Graywolf Press, 2018. p.71.

Walt Whitman excerpt from "Song of Myself," "To A Stranger," "Beat The Drums" Public Domain.

David Whyte "Sweet Darkness" from THE HOUSE of BELONGING. Printed with permission from Many Rivers Press, www.davidwhyte.com. copyright © Many Rivers Press, Langley , Washington USA.

William Wordsworth "I Wandered Lonely As A Cloud." Public Domain.

James Wright " I Was Afraid of Dying" and "The Blessing" from COLLECTED POEMS © 1962 and 1961 by James Wright. Published by Wesleyan University Press and reprinted with permission.

William Butler Yeats "The Lake Isle of Innisfree" Public Domain.

ABOUT THE EDITOR

Deborah has been a teacher of acting for 40 years in the greater New York area. She began at HB Studio in 1981 when Uta Hagen bestowed on her her first technique and scene study classes. She went on to teach at the Ensemble Studio Theater Institute in New York City as well as 12 seasons at its Summer Acting Retreat in Lexington, New York. She has also taught acting at Sarah Lawrence, Fordham University, Mason Gross School of the Arts MFA Acting Conservatory, and the Olmaia Acting Retreat in Tuscany Italy. For 25 years she offered skills study classes at her studio, dh&co, in midtown Manhattan. Deborah continues to work as an actress in and around New York, regionally, as well as numerous new play festivals and conferences. Her theater, television and film credits can be found on her website. www.deborahhedwall.com.